P. W. Raidabaugh

Church History

Text-Book No. 6

P. W. Raidabaugh

Church History
Text-Book No. 6

ISBN/EAN: 9783743398733

Manufactured in Europe, USA, Canada, Australia, Japa

Cover: Foto ©ninafisch / pixelio.de

Manufactured and distributed by brebook publishing software (www.brebook.com)

P. W. Raidabaugh

Church History

COMPILED BY

P. W. RAIDABAUGH.

———•———

CLEVELAND, O.
Publishing House of the Evangelical Association,
LAUER & YOST, AGENTS.
1885.

PREFACE.

The following pages were carefully compiled from the most reliable Church historians. The object is, to embrace short sketches of the most important events of Church history in a connected form, suitable for ready reference; for a detailed account, larger histories must be consulted. For many of the facts in reference to the Reformation in England, the compiler is under obligation of the text book used in the University of Cambridge, prepared for the candidates for the ordinary B. A. Degree, by Rev. Wm. Simpson.

Church History.

COPYRIGHTED BY LAUER & YOST, 1885.

INTRODUCTION.

The sources from which we obtain our information concerning the Church of Christ during the first three centuries are:

1. The four Gospels, which bring down the history to A. D. 33.
2. The Acts of the Apostles, as related by the Evangelist St. Luke, which extends over a period of about 30 years, from A. D. 33 to A. D. 63.
3. The Fathers; to wit: Clement of Rome, Barnabas and Hermas, in the first century; Ignatius, Polycarp, Justin Martyr, Irenæus, and Dionysius of Corinth, in the second century; and Clement of Alexandria, Tertullian, Origen, Cyprian, and Gregory Thaumaturgus, in the third century.
4. Ancient ecclesiastical writers, the earliest of whom is Hegessippus, who flourished about A. D. 170, and the chief of whom is Eusebius, who was probably born at Cæsarea, in Palestine, about A. D. 270.

POLITICAL STATE OF THE WORLD AT CHRIST'S BIRTH.

At the period of Christ's birth the Emperor Augustus reigned at Rome, and his dominion extended over the greater part of the known world. The Roman Empire was then in the utmost perfection as to arts and magnificence; but much declining as to vigor and virtue. Distant nations, submitting to a power too mighty to be withstood, were either governed by Roman Pro-consuls, invested with temporary commissions, or indulged by their conquerors with their own princes and laws, yet reduced to own the claim of Rome to supreme sovereignty, and to enroll themselves in the number of its sons and subjects. The Roman Senate and people, indeed, retained little of authority but the name, for the empire was in reality governed by the victorious and accomplished Augustus. It is said by Orosius that the temple of Janus was shut when Jesus Christ came down to men. Whether this were so or not, it admits of no doubt that the time was eminently free from wars, as compared with preceding ages. The imperial laws were mild, but commotions were not uncommon, in consequence of the extortions and rapacity of provincial governors and tax-gatherers.

RELIGIOUS STATE OF THE WORLD AT CHRIST'S BIRTH.

All nations, except the Jews, were plunged in the grossest superstition and idolatry. Each country had its peculiar gods, whom the people were taught to propitiate with various rites and ceremonies. Religious homage was not confined to the natural world, to departed heroes, or to the improvers of elegance or convenience, but was extended to things inanimate, and to persons merely ideal. Most of the wiser people contemned and ridiculed the popular creeds, but they had nothing else to rest upon, consequently a universal corruption of morals prevailed, and crimes, which at this day cannot be named with decency, were then practiced with impunity.

POLITICAL STATE OF JUDÆA AT CHRIST'S BIRTH.

At the period of our Saviour's birth, Judæa groaned under the tyranny of Herod the Great, by whom the country was harassed, rather than governed. The Jews were not wholly prohibited by their Roman masters from retaining their national laws, and the religion established by Moses. They still had their High Priest, their Priests and Levites, and their Sanhedrim or national council, but the civil power thereof was greatly diminished. With Roman conquest came Roman manners, rites and superstitions: and these were diffused over the whole of Palestine, and blended more or less with those of the Jews. The narrow limits of Palestine could not contain so numerous a nation. Hence, when our Saviour was born, there was hardly any considerable province in which were not found many Jews, who lived by traffic and other arts.

RELIGIOUS STATE OF THE JEWS AT CHRIST'S BIRTH.

The Jews looked for the appearance of some great deliverer—not a spiritual prince, such as the meek and lowly Jesus, but a temporal and warlike hero, who, bringing victories and triumphs in his train, should deliver them from the thraldom of the Roman yoke, and exalt their nation above the rest of the world. They had introduced a variety of superstitions and corruptions into their worship. Religion, according to their ideas, consisted in the practice of the rites appointed by their great lawgiver, and the performance of some external acts of duty towards the Gentiles: the *spirit* of their religion had expired with the Prophets, and nothing survived but a fanatical zeal for the outward observance of the corrupted ceremonial law. They excluded the rest of mankind from the hope of eternal life, and treated them with rigor and contempt. Even the directors in religious concerns, whose superior knowledge should have exalted them above the ignorant multitude, contributed to their errors, by dividing themselves into a great variety of sects, which, though generally agreed upon the ceremonial part of the Jewish religion, were involved in continual disputes.

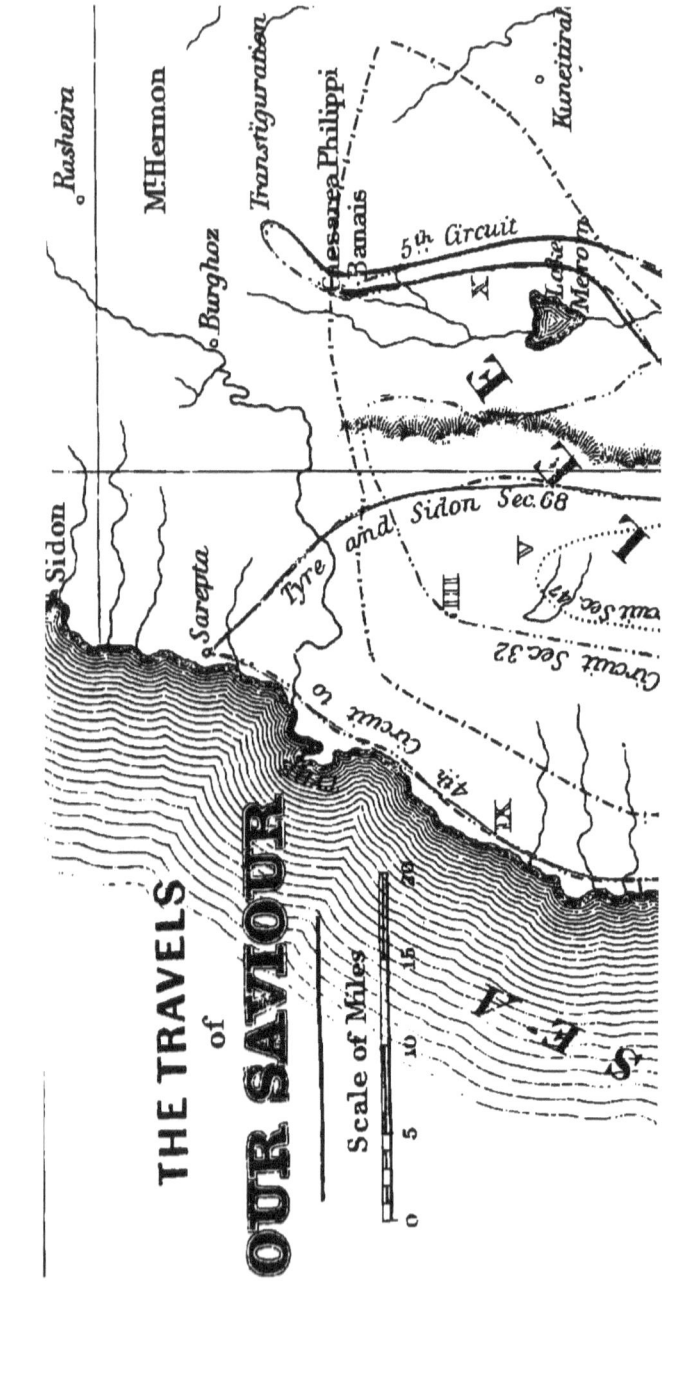

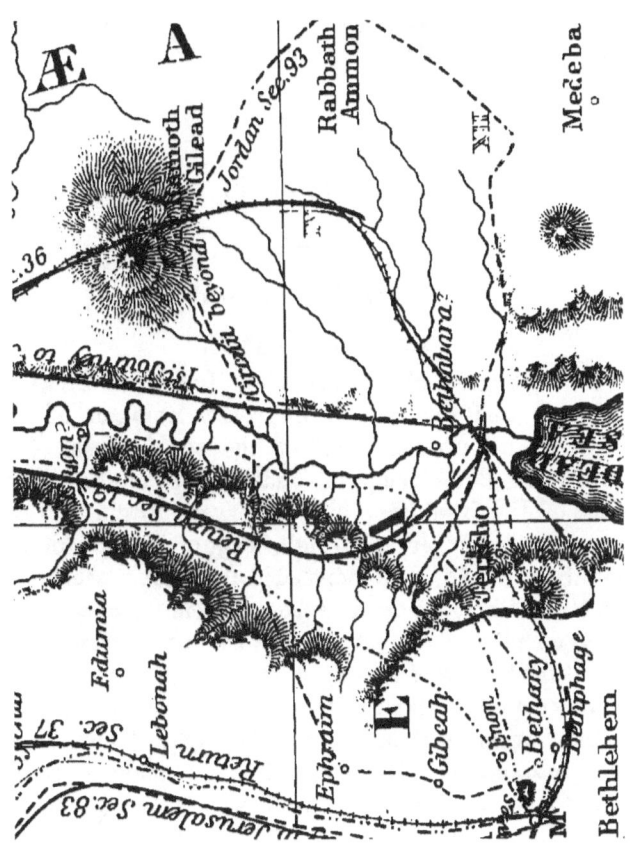

CHURCH HISTORY

CHAPTER I.

THE FIRST CENTURY.

THE LIFE OF CHRIST.

In the 36th year of the reign of Herod the Great, king of the Jews, and the 26th of Augustus, Emperor of Rome, 4000 years after the creation of the world, JESUS CHRIST was born at Bethlehem, in Judæa, the mother city of the tribe of Judah, whither his mother, the Virgin Mary, and his supposed father, Joseph, (both being of the tribe of Judah and family of David), had proceeded from their usual habitation at Nazareth, to render an account of their property, in obedience to an edict of Augustus. The conflux of persons was so great that the houses of reception were full, and the parents of our Lord were constrained to repair to a stable, in which mean place the Saviour was born. On the night of our Saviour's entrance into the world, God was pleased to make a revelation of Him to certain poor shepherds, who were tending their flocks in the very plains where David had often tended his; and on the eighth day, in accordance with the law of Moses, He was circumcised, and called Jesus, as appointed by the angel Gabriel before His conception. Herod, at this time, embarassed with many troubles and conspiracies, was further alarmed by the arrival at Jerusalen of Magi, or astronomers, from Arabia or Chaldea, who, having seen an extraordinary star in their own country, and understanding it to signify the birth of the Messiah promised to the Jews, traveled to the capital of Judæa to worship the new-born Prince, whom they hailed as "King of the Jews." This drove the king into great consternation; he conceived Jesus to be some great temporal prince; and, resolving to destroy his supposed rival in his kingdom, he "sent forth and slew all the children that were in Bethlehem, and in all the coasts thereof, from two years old and under." But God frustrated this design, by warning Joseph in a dream, and causing him to flee into Egypt with the young Child and His mother, where they tarried until the death of Herod. Upon their return from Egypt, the Holy Family proceeded to Nazareth. At twelve years of age we find Jesus disputing publicly with learned Jewish doctors in the temple at Jerusalem, whither His parents had gone to celebrate the Passover. Afterwards, till He was thirty years of age, He dwelt with His parents at Nazareth, as a good and dutiful son. God has not seen fit to give us more particulars concerning the early days of our Saviour. Before entering upon his office of teaching, Jesus chose to receive from John the baptism of repentance, lest, according to His own words, He should seem to have neglected any observance that became a Jew. Being thus prepared for His prophetic office, He was carried into the desert of Judæa, and having been there tempted by the Devil forty days and forty nights, He returned to Nazareth, and commenced his ministry in the district of Galilee. His princi- habitation from this time was at Capernaum, on the sea of Galilee. We need not enter into a particular detail of the ministry of our Lord. His life and actions are to be contem- plated in the writings of the inspired penmen. For about three years, according the most received accounts, amidst great sor- rows, molestation and perils, He instructed the Jewish people in the counsels and purposes the Most High; and at the end of that period, having preached the Gospel, appointed the twelve Apostles as the founders of the Church, and confirmed His Divine mission by a series of stupendous miracles, He was betrayed to His enemies by Judas, and dragged before the High Priest, Caiaphas, and then before the Sanhedrim, on a charge of blasphemy. But the Jewish Council having no longer the power of life and death, He was accused of sedition and treason against Cæsar, before the Roman Governor, Pontius Pilate, who reluctantly condemned Him to death. Having come into the world to make expiation for the sins of men, He voluntarily submitted to be nailed to a cross, on which he yielded up His spotless soul to God. His body was buried by Joseph of Arimathea; but on the third day He rose again from the dead. He now continued forty days with His disciples, instructing them more fully concerning the nature of His kingdom. At length, having led them forth to Bethany, He was taken up from their presence into the glories of Heaven.

NOTE.—About four months after our Lord's entrance upon His ministry, He made choice of twelve persons, according to the number of the tribes of Israel, to be witnesses of His actions and discourses; and, after his departure out of the world, to be propagators of His Gospel. These He called *Apostles*, which imports "messengers" or "ambassadors." They were plebeians, mostly fishermen, poor and illiterate; for He employed not the rich, the eloquent or the learned, lest the success of their mission should be ascribed to human and natural causes. The men thus honored by our Saviour were the following:—

(1) *Simon*, or *Simeon*, named *Peter*, the eldest of all the Apostles, for which reason, probably, histories give him precedency. He was a native of Bethsaida, in Galilee.

(2) *Andrew*, brother of Peter.

(3) *James*, commonly called *James the Great*, son of Zebedee and Solome, was born at Bethsaida.

(4) *John*, younger brother of *James the Great*, and the youngest of all the Apostles. These two were surnamed by our Lord *Boanerges*, or the *Sons of Thunder*, on account of their brave and resolute tempers.

(5) *Philip*, who was called first by our Saviour, was a native of Bethsaida.

(6) *Bartholomew*, probably the same with Nathaniel. (cf. Matt. 10. 3; Mark 3. 18; Luke 6. 14; with John 1. 45).

(7) *Matthew*, called also *Levi*, son of Alpheus, a rich publican, or taxgatherer, of Capernaum.

(8) *Thomas*, called also *Didymus*, a Galilean, of mean parentage.

(9) *James*, commonly distinguished by the name of *James the Less*, the son of Alpheus, or Cleopas, and Mary, sister of the blessed Virgin, and therefore the cousin-german of Christ; upon which account, according to the Jewish custom, he is often called the brother of our Lord (Gal. 1. 19).

(10) *Simon*, distinguished from Simon-Peter by the *equivalent* titles Cananite (Matt. 10. 4; Mark 3. 18), and Zealot, (Luke 6. 15; Acts 1. 13). Whether he was that Simon who was brother to James the Less is uncertain.

(11) *Judas*, commonly called *Jude*, and sometimes *Thaddæus* and *Lebbæus* brother to James the Less.

(12) *Judas*, surnamed *Iscariot*, *i. e.*, man of Kerioth, who betrayed our Lord.

FIRST YEAR OF THE CHURCH.

According to the chronology which we have adopted, the conversion of Saul took place in the first year of the Church, dating the foundation thereof from the day of Pentecost, A. D. 29. The following events, as related by St. Luke, had already occurred : — Matthias having been elected and numbered with the Apostles, and the Holy Spirit having descended upon them, 3,000 persons were converted by the preaching of Peter; the cripple was healed at the beautiful gate of the Temple by Peter and John, who were imprisoned in consequence of the success attending a discourse of the former, but were discharged next day: Ananias and Sapphira fell down dead at the rebuke of Peter, for lying to the Holy Ghost. The Apostles were then imprisoned, but set at liberty on the advice of Gamaliel, seven Deacons were then chosen to perform certain civil and ecclesiastical duties. Persecution followed the increase in the number of disciples which now took place, and Stephen died, the first Christian martyr. The persecution grew more fierce, and the Church was dispersed; Philip fled to Samaria, where he baptized Simon Magus, the Ethiopian eunuch, and many others, and Peter and John went there to complete the work which Philip had begun, by conferring the gifts of the Holy Ghost; the religion was now spread, and Saul was converted to the Christian faith, while on his way to persecute the Church at Damascus

PROGRESS OF THE GOSPEL.

We may suppose that the Gospel continued to advance, notwithstanding the difficulties which it had to encounter. As addressed to the Jews, these difficulties may be referred to the following causes: — (1) It was adverse to the opinions upon which their national hopes were founded, for they clung to the expectation of a temporal Prince, who was to raise their nation above every other. (2) Without repealing the Levitical code, it lowered its estimation greatly, and decried the long-esteemed merit of ritual zeal. (3) It represented the crucifixion of its Founder as a cruel and unjust murder. On the other hand, it was not without circumstances favorable to its progress. The Roman government was indifferent to the religious disputes of the Jews, and consequently gave no encouragement to the opposition to the spread of the Gospel. It was bent on preserving peace; and the Jewish dignitaries for the most part knew their own interest too well to neglect so manifest a means of ingratiating themselves with their Roman masters, as that of endeavoring to abate a disposition to turbulence in consequence of religious differences. The work of evangelization, then, advanced. In various parts of Palestine, no doubt, Churches were established by the Apostles; and as each of these was founded, the care of it seems to have been committed to one or more ministers, the Apostles themselves continuing to be the superintendents of it, and traveling from place to place, wherever they had planted a Church. It is thought that there were also other ministers, in addition to those specially appointed to the different Churches, whose office it was to go about in the country, discharging their spiritual duties. These were called *Evangelists*. Mark and Luke were probably of this class, in addition to their being Evangelists in the modern acceptation of the term; as being the authors of written Gospels. Thus matters proceeded for some few years, during which there is little for the historian to record out of the scanty materials that have come down to us.

CALIGULA.

Tiberius having been murdered, after a reign of 22 years, was succeeded in the year 37, by Caius Caligula, son of his nephew, Germanicus. Caligula began his reign at the age of 25 with all clemency and regularity; but his promising qualities soon vanished, and he acquired such a complication of enormities that he became one of the worst monsters that ever trod the earth. For a few years he proved a terrible scourge to the Romans.

In the reign of Caligula the Jews were reduced to such difficulties and dangers by the pride of the Emperor that they had little time to think of persecuting the Christians; and to this may in a great measure be attributed the peace which the Church enjoyed at this time, and the progress which the Gospel made. The Emperor expected that all nations should adore him as a god, and sent express orders to Petronius, the successor of Vitellius in Syria, to dedicate a large and costly image to him, and set it up in the very Temple at Jerusalem, which was henceforth to be called "the Temple of illustrious Caius and propitious Jupiter." This outrage kept Judæa in a ferment, and Petronius was so affected by the distress of the Jews that he deferred the dedication of the image, and the Jews were finally successful in their resistance, through the mediation of Agrippa.

THE CHURCH AT ANTIOCH.

During these transactions the Church flourished exceedingly, and the Gospel spread among the Jews in all parts. But probably there was no place, except Jerusalem, where the new religion made such great progress as it did in Antioch, the capital of Syria. Rejecting the idea of some that Peter founded a bishopric here in the year 39, there is no doubt that in the first few years of Christianity, the Church at Antioch (founded probably after the dispersion upon the death of Stephen) was one of the most flourishing. It was long before it was visited by any one from Jerusalem. The deposition of Pilate, however, and the annexation of Judæa to the Presidentship of Syria, brought the two cities into closer connection, and established more regular communication between them. About the year 41 a report of the number of converts at Antioch having reached the ears of the Apostles at Jerusalem, they sent Barnabas to visit the Christians there. Barnabas, encouraged by the favorable prospect, proceeded to Tarsus to engage the services of Saul, who came and remained at Antioch for a whole year, during which time the Gospel seems to have spread rapidly among all ranks (Acts 11. 22). It was the pivot on which the Church of the Gentiles more especially revolved. "And the disciples were called *Christians* first in Antioch" (Acts 11. 26).

CALL OF THE GENTILES.

For several years after the Ascension, the Gospel was preached only to the Jews. The Apostles, it is true, had received commission to baptize all nations, but they understood it only of the *Jews* of all nations. But now God thought fit to open a door to the Gentiles. A special revelation upon the subject was made to Peter, who baptized the first Gentile convert, namely, Cornelius, a Roman Centurion quartered at Cæsarea, the usual residence of the governor. Cornelius was a devout man who feared God (Acts 10. 2), and was probably distinct from the idolatrous Gentiles on the one hand, and from Proselytes (with whom he is often ranked) on the other.

DEATH OF JAMES.

During the prevalence of the famine foretold by Agabus, the the Christians at Jerusalem, who for ten years before had met with no great disturbance, suffered from a sharp persecution raised against them by King Herod Agrippa. Desirous to ingratiate himself with the Jews, he struck at the Apostles themselves, and began with James, son of Zebedee and brother of John, whom he "killed with the sword" (Acts 12. 2). Thus fell James, surnamed the Great, the Apostolic proto-martyr, the first of that number who gained the crown. Clemens Alexandrinus relates that his accuser, convinced by the extraordinary courage and constancy displayed by James at his trial, publicly professed himself a Christian, and was beheaded at the same time as the Apostle. The death of James was so gratifying to the Jews, that Agrippa proceeded to apprehend Peter also, and committed him to prison, designing to have him executed immediately after the feast of the Passover. But Peter was miraculously delivered by an angel, and withdrew himself to a place of greater security. Upon this the King, having commanded the keepers of the prison to be put to death, departed from Jerusalem to Cæsarea, where he was seized with a loathsome malady, and died miserably, after enduring exquisite torments in his bowels for five days.

THE SERVICE OF THE GENTILES.

About the time of Agrippa's death, Saul and Barnabas, having disposed of their contributions at Jerusalem, returned to Antioch, where a divine revelation was made that these two should be set apart for the service of the Gentiles (Acts 13. 2). They were accordingly ordained to be ministers of the uncircumcision. From this joint commission Barnabas also obtained the name of Apostle; St. Jerome calls him the fourteenth Apostle, and the Greek and Latin Church ever honored him as much.

DISPERSION OF THE APOSTLES.

For twelve years after the Ascension all the Apostles, except St. Paul (whose labors are related in the Acts), confined themselves in a manner to Palestine; but now the time was come when, according to their Lord's command, they were to disperse and preach the Gospel in all parts of the world. Some suppose that before their departure they composed the Apostles' Creed and the Apostles' Canons; but most learned men are satisfied that both belong to later times. The part of the world in which each Apostle carried on his labors is involved in doubt and uncertainty. The general opinion is that *Peter* went into Pontus, Galatia, and Lower Asia. *Andrew* had Scythia and Sogdiana alloted to him; though afterwards he is supposed to have turned towards Greece, and founded the Bishopric of Byzantium. *John's* portion was partly the same as Peter's, namely, Lesser Asia, fixing his residence chiefly at Ephesus; but he remained in Jerusalem till after the death of Mary, the mother of Jesus. *Philip* had upper Asia, with parts of Scythia and Colchis. Arabia Felix was allotted to *Bartholomew*, into which parts he carried the Gospel of St. Matthew. *Matthew* himself preached in Asiatic Ethiopia, Chaldæa, Persia, and Parthia, but Parthia was more particularly allotted to *Thomas*, who also preached to the Hyrcanians, Bactrians, and Indians. *James the Less*, being Bishop of Jerusalem, continued principally in that city. *Simon* had Egypt, Cyrene, Libya, and and Mauritania. *Jude* had Syria and Mesopotamia. *Matthias* had Cappadocia and Colchis.

ST. PAUL'S APOSTOLIC JOURNEYS.

Of the travels and actions of the Apostles we have but a very short and uncertain account. The narrative of St. Luke, leaving the rest of the Apostles, proceeds with the separate memoirs of Saul, the thirteenth Apostle. Having been separated with Barnabas to the ministry of the Gentiles, these two, accompanied by John Mark, the nephew of Barnabas, set out from Antioch (in Syria) to Cyprus, where they converted Sergius Paulus, the Roman Governor. and Saul adopted the name of Paul. From Cyprus, Paul proceeded to Perga in Pamphilia, and having suffered various persecutions at Antioch (in Pisidia), Iconium, and Lystra, he returned to Antioch. After abiding here some time, the Council at Jerusalem having been held meanwhile, Paul, accompanied by Luke, proceeded on a second journey through Asia Minor to Ephesus, and, crossing the Ægean sea, visited Philippi, where he was whipped and imprisoned; then Thessalonica, where the Jews raised such commotions as obliged him to escape to Athens; then Corinth, where he was brought before the Roman tribunal, but dismissed, from the contempt the magistrate entertained for the Jewish controversies, of which he accounted Christianity to be one; then Ephesus, and so through Asia Minor to Jerusalem. After this Paul again visited Antioch, and then Ephesus, passing through Asia Minor: at Ephesus, where he daily ministered for two years, he nearly lost his life, in a commotion raised by Demetrius, the silversmith, in consequence of the decline of the trade in images, he was driven from Ephesus only to renew his labors in Greece, where, after proceeding as far as the borders of Illyricum, he revisited Corinth, and, in consequence of a conspiracy of the Jews, traced his steps back through Macedonia to Philippi; whence he took shipping to Jerusalem, reaching that city in time for the feast of Pentecost, after an absence of nearly five years.

JUDAIZING CHRISTIANS.— COUNCIL AT JERUSALEM.

The principle that it was not necessary for a heathen to conform to the Mosaic law, before or after his conversion to Christianity, was established by Paul and Barnabas during their first journey. This was not the doctrine of a large party in the Church at Jerusalem, whatever was the practice of the Church at Antioch; for upon the return of Paul and Barnabas to the latter city, they found the Gentile converts greatly distressed, in consequence of some of the teaching of some of the party from Jerusalem, that unless they observed circumcision and the Mosaic institutions, they could never be saved (Acts 15. 1). This was so complete a subversion of the doctrine of salvation by Christ, that the teaching could not be for a moment admitted. After many conferences and disputations, it was judged requisite to send a deputation to consult the Apostles and Presbyters at Jerusalem, and to bring back a definite sentence concerning this important question. Accordingly, early next year, Paul and Barnabas, taking with them Titus and others, repaired to Jerusalem for this purpose. James, Peter, and John were at this time in Jerusalem, and it was resolved to appoint an assembly of themselves and the Presbyters to settle this matter. At this assembly James, as the head of the Church at Jerusalem, appears to have presided. After " much disputing," Peter spake in favor of the Gentiles, showing that it is only "through the grace of our Lord Jesus Christ we shall be saved" (Acts 15. 11). Paul and Barnabas followed to the same effect, "declaring what miracles God had wrought among the Gentiles by them" (Acts 15. 12.); and then James, in the name of the Council, gave sentence that the Jewish rites ought not to be imposed upon believing Gentiles; but, that the zealous Jew might have no offence, it was agreed that the Gentile converts should abstain from four things: — 1) From what had been offered in sacrifice to idols, because the contrary might seem a participation in the idolatry; 2) from fornication, which the Gentiles accounted little or no crime; 3) from strangled meat, which was extremely odious to the Jews; and 4) from blood, which was supposed to be forbidden to affright men from cruelty and bloodshed. The decree, having been formally written out, was delivered by Paul and Barnabas, who, accompanied by Judas and Silvanus, returned to Antioch.

CERINTHUS AND THE CERINTHIANS.

Epiphanius, bishop of Salamina in Cyprus, the author of a work entitled *Contra Octaginta Hæreses*, tells us (128. ¿ 3.) that the noted heretic, Cerinthus, was the ringleader of the faction at Antioch, which disturbed the Church there, upon the question of the circumcision of Gentile converts; but others assign so late a date as the end of the century to his notoriety. He was by birth a Jew, but was initiated in letters and philosophy at Alexandria. His heresy was a species of Gnosticism, modified so as to seem not quite inconsistent with Jewish opinions. Thus, he allowed that the creator of the world was lawgiver of

the Jews, and a being endowed at first with the greatest virtue; but asserted that he derived his power from the supreme God: and that he had by degrees fallen from his native dignity and virtue — that in order to destroy his corruptive empire, the Supreme God had commissioned one of his glorious Œons, whose name was *Christ*, to descend upon earth, and that when Jesus was baptized in the Jordan, *Christ* entered into the body of the man *Jesus* (Christ and Jesus being two distinct beings) which was crucified, but that Christ had not suffered, but ascended into Heaven. Cerinthus required his followers to retain in part of the Mosaic law, but to regulate their lives by the example of Christ; and taught that a resurrection of the body would take place, after which Christ would reign upon earth with his faithful disciples a thousand years, which would be spent in the basest sensual indulgencies. In the doctrine of a millennium he partly agreed with Justin Martyr, Irenæus, Tertullian, and others; but these celebrated persons did not share in his gross notions of the millennial sabbath. This mixture of Judaism and Oriental philosophy made many converts, and the Cerinthians soon became numerous. They admitted a part of St. Matthew's Gospel, but rejected the rest, and held the epistles of St. Paul in great abhorrence. Irenæus says that St. John wrote his Gospel "to root out the erroneous doctrine which had been spread by Cerinthus."

DISAGREEMENT BETWEEN PAUL AND PETER.

Not long after the Council at Jerusalem, Peter came to Antioch, and for a time mixed freely with the Gentile converts; but subsequently, from fear of offending certain Jewish Christians, began to separate himself from them, which tended to confirm the Jews in their darling opinions, and to fill the Gentiles with new doubts and scruples. Even Barnabas followed the example of Peter; but Paul stood firm, and reproved Peter in the face of the whole Church, lest the weaker brethren should be more led away to attach importance to unessential points. Peter bore the reproof with patience, and no doubt amended his carriage. This is the last time that we read of Peter in the Holy Scriptures (Galatians 2. 11, 19). It is supposed, though it cannot be demonstrated from Scripture, that he went to Rome; where he is said to have encountered Simon Magus again. Here it is generally thought that he suffered martyrdom about A. D. 68.

NERO.

In the year 54 Claudius was poisoned by his wife, Agrippina, after a reign of about thirteen years and a half. He was succeeded by Nero, son of Agrippina by a former marriage with C. Domitius Ahenobarbus, at this time only 17 years of age. Nero showed himself, in the beginning of his reign, just, liberal, and merciful, but was afterwards a monster of cruelty and barbarity. He was the first Emperor that persecuted the Christian Church.

ST. PAUL'S IMPRISONMENT.

Paul had not been many days at Jerusalem after his third journey, when the Jews, with whom the city was crowded in consequence of the feast, forced him out of the Temple, and would have destroyed him, had not the sudden presence of the Roman guard, under Claudius Lysias, from the tower of Antonia, rescued him out of their hands. It was the duty of this guard to preserve the public peace, and to this, and not to any favor of the Apostle, must the interposition be attributed; for no sooner had Lysias secured his person in the fortress than he began to examine him by torture. But on finding that Paul was a Roman citizen, he sent him to Cæsarea, where the Procurator Felix usually resided. Here he was detained for two years; but upon Festus succeeding Felix in the office of the Procurator, in the year 60, declining to have his case heard at Jerusalem, and appealing to the Emperor as a Roman, he was sent to Rome, accompanied by Luke, Aristarchus, Trophimus, and some others. After a tempestuous voyage they were wrecked on the Island of Melita, now called Malta, where they stayed three months, planting a church and making many converts. In the early part of the spring they left Malta, and landed at Puteoli, a part of Campania, whence they proceeded shortly to Rome, the Christians of that city having come out to meet them, some as far as Appii Forum a distance of fifty-one miles. For two years he received all that came to him, in a house which he was permitted to hire; he was under the restraint of a soldier chained to him by the arm, but he preached the kingdom of God freely during his imprisonment.

ST. PAUL'S RELEASE.

After Paul had been above four years a prisoner of the Roman power, of which the latter two were passed at Rome, he was set at liberty, being found not guilty of the breach of any Roman law. We have no certain account of the subsequent career of Paul. He is said by Clemens Romanus to have travelled to *the utmost bounds of the west;* and by Theodoret to have brought the salvation to the *islands that lie in the Ocean.* So that it has been supposed that, in the course of his zealous endeavors to extend the Gospel, he travelled westward as far as Spain, or Gaul, or even Britain. His martyrdom will be spoken of immediately.

CHRISTIANITY AT ROME.

When St. Paul arrived at Rome, there were many Christians in the city, for St. Luke says, "When the brethren heard of us, they came to meet us, as far as Appii Forum and the Three Taverns" (Acts 27. 15). Christianity was probably introduced into Rome by the "strangers of Rome, Jews and proselytes" (Acts 2. 10.), who listened to the preaching of Peter on the day of Pentecost. St. Paul's preaching at Rome during his first imprisonment was abundantly fruitful: his principal converts were probably Gentiles, some of them being people of rank and fortune, and even members of the Emperor's household: "All saints salute you, chiefly they that are of Cæsar's household" (Phil. 4. 22). St. Paul seems to have been the first Apostle who visited Rome.

CHRISTIANITY AT ALEXANDRIA.

We have no authentic account of the introduction of Christianity into Alexandria; but as dwellers in Egypt, and in the parts of Lybia about Cyrene, were in Jerusalem when the Holy Spirit came down upon the Apostles on the day of Pentecost, it is probable that the doctrine of the Cross was carried thither upon the return of these to their homes. The first Bishop was Mark, the Evangelist, by whom the Church there is supposed to have been founded. There is a tradition that he suffered martyrdom at Alexandria in the first general persecution, about the year 67 A. D.; but the probability is that he died a natural death in the eigth year of Nero's reign. Annianus succeeded him in the administration of the Alexandrian Church.

FREEDOM FROM ROMAN PERSECUTION.

It does not appear that public laws were enacted against Christianity till the reign of Nero. The reason for this may be, that the converts to Christianity were regarded only as a Jewish sect, who had seceded from their brethren on account of some difference of opinion of trifling importance; and as the Romans were not accustomed to trouble individuals on account of their religion, and as they suffered the Jews in particular to live according to their own laws, it is not likely they would pay much attention to what they regarded as the intestine quarrels of the Jews. But in the time of Nero, Christianity had acquired considerable extent and stability, and its steady and uniform opposition to heathen superstition would be sure to raise up enemies interested in its suppression.

CAUSES OF ROMAN PERSECUTION.

Independent of the general cause of persecution arising from the steady progress of Christianity, the following particular causes may be mentioned: — (1) The Christians contemned the religion of the State, which was closely connected with the Roman Government; and the Romans, although they tolerated religions from which the commonwealth had nothing to fear, would not suffer the ancient religion of their nation to be derided, and the people to be withdrawn from it. Yet these things the Christians dared to do. They also assailed the religions of all other nations. Hence, they were concluded to be unfriendly to public peace. (2) The Christian worship had no sacrifices, temples, statues, or oracles: hence its professors were deemed Atheists, and by the Roman laws Atheists were regarded as the pest of human society. Moreover, the worship of so many Pagan deities afforded support to great numbers, who where in danger of coming to want if Christianity should prevail. Such were the priests, soothsayers, statuaries, players, gladiators, and others who depended for a livelihood on the worship of the heathen gods, or on spectacles which the

Christians abhorred. (3) Their cautious method of performing the offices of religion, dictated at first by fear of persecution, caused horrid calumnies to be circulated against them. Thyestean banquets, promiscuous intercourse of the sexes, and magical rites were popularly imputed to them, and it was believed that national calamities were sent by the gods, because the Christians, who contemned their authority, were tolerated.

FIRST GENERAL PERSECUTION.

Under these circumstances, it is not wonderful that Nero, who had now fallen into monstrous vices, should endeavor to transfer to the Christians the guilt of which he was strongly suspected, that of having set fire to Rome, in the year 64. With this view, he inflicted upon them the most exquisite tortures. Some, as Tacitus informs us, were crucified; others impaled; some thrown to wild beasts; and others wrapped in garments dipped in pitch, and burned as torches to illuminate the night. In this persecution it is supposed that Paul and Peter suffered martyrdom at Rome; but there is a controversy about the year, some contending that it was 64, and others 67 or 68. Paul, as a Roman citizen, was beheaded; but Peter, not being a citizen of Rome, was crucified as a common criminal. It is said they both suffered on the same day. Linus, the first Bishop of Rome, is also thought to have suffered about this time. The first persecution began in the year 64 and ended in 68. Whether it extended beyond the immediate neighborhood of Rome has been a subject of dispute. Though not, perhaps, officially sanctioned beyond the limits of Rome, we meet with notices of martyrs who are said to have suffered in other countries.

EFFECTS OF PERSECUTION.

This and other Pagan persecutions were probably not upon the whole unfavorable to the progress of Christianity. For, their extreme barbarity was not only revolting to the spectators, but gave fortitude to the sufferers, whose constancy in torture won the admiration of the best part of the heathen, and convinced them of the sincerity of the Christians. And, in addition to this, Christians were dispersed into distant lands by the cruelties practiced against them, and carried with them the doctrines of the Gospel to places which would otherwise have long remained without them.

THE JEWISH WAR.

Towards the latter end of the year in which Rome was burnt, Gessius Florus succeeded Albinus as Procurator of Judæa. The rapacity and oppression of this man created great discontent among the Jews, who at length broke out into open rebellion against Rome, in the year 66. After various skirmishes and massacres, Cestius Gallus, Governor of Syria, advanced against Judæa and Jerusalem, but was defeated with considerable loss. This was the signal for open war, the management of which war was subsequently entrusted to Vespasian, who laid siege to Jerusalem. In the year 69, Vespasian was proclaimed Emperor, and some time afterwards his son Titus took the command of the besieging army. Vespasian held the empire for ten years, during which time the Christians lived in peace; and no one, as far as we know, was put to death on account of his religion. Jerusalem, with its Temple, was taken and entirely destroyed by Titus in the year 72, and the capitation tax which each Jew used to pay for the maintenance of the Temple, was ordered to be paid henceforward to the capitol of Rome. In this war, which lasted for nearly six years, upwards of a million Jews are said to have perished, and though, for fear of a rival, he is said to have sought out the descendants of David, yet it has been asserted that every Christian escaped. Here ended the temporal State and economy of the Jews, who, from that time to the present, have been dispersed throughout all parts of the world.

THE CHSISTIANS AT PELLA—NAZARENES AND EBIONITES.

Our Lord had given the Christians a warning to flee from Jerusalem when they should see it compassed with armies (Matt. 24. 15, 21.) Accordingly, in the early part of the Jewish war, they fled, accompanied by Symeon, their Bishop, to Pella, a little city on the eastern side of the Jordan, belonging to Agrippa's dominions. On the conclusion of the war, many of them, accompanied by their Bishop, returned to Jerusalem, where they set up again a Christian Church, and, discarding Jewish forms and ceremonies, restored the doctrines of the Gospel. Many, however, remained at Pella; and from them arose the two sects of the *Nazarenes* and *Ebionites*. The former were most likely not heretics, but Christians, who continued to adhere to the ceremonies of the Mosaic law, and were consequently somewhat slightingly spoken of by their brethren, now that the destruction of Jerusalem and the Temple had weakened the respect for the law, and diminished the number of Judaizing Christians. The Ebionites, on the other hand, were decidedly heretical, entertaining certain Gnostic errors. They denied the divinity of our Saviour, believing that he was born of human parents, and that Christ descended upon Jesus at his baptism; enjoined the observation of the law as necessary to salvation; received part of the Old Testament, but utterly rejected the New Testament, except a Hebrew Gospel of St. Matthew, from which, however, they expunged everything relating to the miraculous conception and birth of Christ. They relied much on apocryphal Scriptures, and condemned Paul as an apostate, for having proved the dissolution of the Mosaic law.

TITUS.

Vespasian was succeeded in the year 79 by his son Titus, who had a bad reputation on account of his severity and voluptuous life. But when he became charged with the burden of the empire, his virtues displayed themselves, and he ruled with moderation and advantage to the people. Although Linus, first Bishop of Rome, is said by some to have suffered in Nero's persecution, others assign his martyrdom to the reign of Titus. It does not appear, however, that the Christians were generally molested, either in this or the preceding reign.

DOMITIAN.

After a reign of a little more than two years, Titus was succeeded by his younger brother Domitian, not inferior to Nero in baseness of character. In the early part of his reign Domitian was probably too much engaged in cruelties against his heathen subjects to allow of much consideration being bestowed upon the Christians; but about the year 94 he began to exact with great severity the tax levied upon the Jews (with whom the Christians were confounded), towards the maintenance of the Capitol at Rome. Moreover, in addition to the general causes of persecution, he was excited to acts of cruelty against the Christians by political motives, for he had heard that a person would come from the line of David, who would attempt a revolution, and produce a commotion in the empire. He particularly commanded, therefore, that the posterity of David should be sought out and put to death. In pursuance of his command, two grandchildren of the Apostle Jude — the "brother" of our Lord, as he is called — were brought before him. Their poverty and humility, together with the declaration that Christ's kingdom was not of this world, convinced him that he had nothing to fear from them, and consequently they were dismissed. Hegesippus and Tertullian assert that Domitian immediately published a decree, terminating the persecution; but others are of opinion that the persecution was continued until the Emperor's death in the year 96, wider in its reach, but of less severity than that instituted by Nero. It raged throughout the Roman empire against both Jews and Christians. The principal Christian martyrs named are Flavius Clemens, uncle to the Emperor, and Consul the preceding year, and Acilius Glabro, who were put to death on a charge of atheism, with which Christianity was sometimes confounded. Flavia Domitilla, the wife of Flavius Clemens, was also banished. But the most memorable incident in the Domitian persecution was the suffering of the Apostle John, at that time residing at Ephesus, whither he went to oppose the spread of the Gnostic heresy. Charged as a disturber of the public peace, he was sent bound to Rome, where he was treated with all the cruelty that rage could suggest. Tertullian, who lived in the second century, relates that he was cast into a cauldron of boiling oil, in front of one of the gates of Rome, called *Porta Latina*, from which he came unhurt. This tale is, however, discredited; but John was banished to Patmos, an island in the Ægean Sea, there to be employed in digging mines. In this place God gave him a prospect of the future state of Christianity, in those Revelations which are transmitted to us in the book of that name.

THE NICOLAITAN HERESY.

In the reign of Domitian there appeared the sect of the Nicolaitans, who pretended to derive their name from Nicolas, the deacon. They are mentioned in the Revelations of St. John (2. 6, 14, 15), where the angel of God reproaches the Church of Pergamos with harboring persons of this denomination. It is true that they are not there taxed with errors in matters of *faith*, but only with licentious *conduct*, and a disregard of the injunction of the Apostles to abstain from meats offered to idols. But Irenæus, Tertullian, Clemens Alexandrinus, and others accuse them of partaking of the Gnostic opinions concerning two principles, the Œons, and the origin of this present world. It is doubtful, however, whether on this point there be not some confusion between the Apocaliptical Nicolaitans, and a Gnostic sect of the second century, founded by a man named Nicholaus.

NERVA.

Domitian, who was stabbed by Stephanus, in the year 96, was succeeded by Nerva. One of the earliest acts of the new Emperor was to rescind the decrees of his predecessor, particularly recalling the banished Jews and Christians, restoring confiscated property, and permitting them the practice of their religion. Having then issued a proclamation, forbidding the Christians to be persecuted solely upon account of their religion, the Church increased greatly during his reign; nevertheless it was not without martyrs. Timothy, Bishop of Ephesus, suffered in the early part of the year 97. He is said to have opposed the celebration of a festival by the votaries of Diana, which so enraged the people that they attacked him with clubs and stones, two days after which he died of his wounds.

THE APOSTLE JOHN.

We have seen that John was banished to Patmos by Domitian. Soon after the death of Timothy, Bishop of Ephesus, he took advantage of Nerva's edict and returned to Ephesus, and was invested with the care of the Church at that place. It is supposed that he wrote his Epistles and Gospel, as well as the Revelations, towards the close of his life, either during his imprisonment at Patmos, or after his return to Ephesus. Many suppose St. John's Gospel to have been the last of Holy Scriptures. The other three Evangelists had shown the humanity of Jesus Christ — St. John manifested his Divinity. Two reasons are resigned by the ancients for the writing of this Gospel. First to refute the Gnostic heresy, which denied our Saviour's Divinity, and His existence before His incarnation; wherefore St. John begins asserting, "In the beginning was the Word, and the Word was with God, and the Word was God." Secondly, to confirm the history of the other three Evangelists, and supply their omissions. St. John, who outlived the other Apostles by many years, is said to have died at Ephesus, in the reign of Trajan, about the end of the first century, having attained the age of 100 years or more. Of his last years, which were spent in the superintendence of the Ephesian Church, some traditions have been preserved.

CHAPTER II.

From the death of John the Evangelist till the rise of Monachism.—A. D. 100–249.

I. THE SECOND CENTURY.

THIRD PERSECUTION.

Nerva died in the year 98, and was succeeded by Trajan, a Spaniard by birth. The character of Trajan was for the most part that of a mild and virtuous prince; so that, centuries after his death, the highest wish that could be expressed in favor of a new Emperor was that he might be 'better than Trajan;' yet his zeal for Paganism proved detrimental to the religion of Christ, and his character is sullied by the martyrdom of Ignatius, who was sentenced to death by the Emperor in person. During Nerva's reign, Christianity had been allowed to spread with little or no opposition, and the fury of its enemies, for a while held in check, was ready to burst forth upon that Emperor's death, though there is no evidence of any persecution at Rome yet. Popular tumults against the Christians were therefore common in Trajan's reign, especially in the eastern part of the empire. Symeon, second Bishop of Jerusalem, is supposed to have suffered martyrdom in this reign, about the year 104. His death may be attributed to the jealousy of the Roman government against the line of David, which both Vespasian and Domitian had endeavored to extirpate. He was denounced to Atticus, the President of Syria, by some Jewish sect, for being of the posterity of the kings of Judah; and after enduring tortures with a fortitude which extorted the admiration of his enemies, he was crucified in the 120th year of his age. Clement is also said to have suffered in the reign of Trajan. The Emperor himself does not appear to have been personally connected with the death of either of these eminent persons.

MILLENNIUM.

Papias, Bishop of Hierapolis in Phrygia, and one of St. John's disciples, flourished in the reign of Trajan. He was the first propagator of the doctrine of a Millennium, or reign of Christ upon earth for a thousand years, when there would be a first resurrection of the just, previously to the final resurrection of all men at the day of judgment. Papias, having been a disciple of St. John, was supposed best to know the Apostle's mind as to the thousand years mentioned in Revelations (ch. 20). Hence, the doctrine of a Millennium was much in vogue for two or three centuries, and those who held it were much termed Millennarians and Chiliasts. It was held, not only by the Gnostic heretics, especially the Cerinthians, and by the Montanists, but likewise by Justin Martyr, Irenæus, Tertullian, and others; but the notions of these latter were not of that gross and sensual kind which have been ascribed to Cerinthus and his followers. Origen powerfully refuted the millennarian doctrine.

SATURNINUS.

Towards the latter end of Trajan's reign, Saturninus of Antioch in Syria, began to propagate there the absurdities of Simon Magus and Menander, adding others of his own.

He supposed two first causes of all things, the good God, and matter, which is in its nature evil; and affirmed that the world and men were made by seven Œons, or angelic natures—the God of the Jews being their chief; and that God, pleased with the work, imparted rational souls to the men, who before had only animal life. In opposition to these good men, the Lord of matter, or Satan, with whom the angels carried on an unceasing warfare, produced an unholy race, to whom he imparted a malignant soul. Hence the difference between good and bad men. The Old Testament, he held, was in part given by the seven angels (especially by the God of the Jews), and in part by Satan. The creators of the world having revolted from the supreme God, he sent down the Œon Nous ($νοῦς$, *Mind*) or Christ, clothed with a fallacious body, to destroy the kingdom of the Lord of matter, and point out to the hard and difficult way of returning back to God. Saturninus denied the resurrection of the body, and inculcated abstinence from marriage. By this austerity of life and great show of virtue, he drew many after him. The sect, however, did not extend beyond Syria, and soon came to an end.

BASILIDES.

Basilides of Syria, another disciple of Menander, flourished at Alexandria, whilst Saturninus flourished in Syria. Like other Gnostics, his system combined the principles of Emanation and Dualism. He enlarged upon the innovations of former heretics. He taught that from the supreme God were evolved by successive generations, seven intelligences, or personified existences, viz., Understanding, Word, Thought, Wisdom, Power, Righteousness, and Peace. These gave birth to a second order of spirits; the second to a third; and the course of emanations continued till there were 365 orders, each consisting of seven spirits, and each with a heaven of its own. The number of the heavens was expressed by the word Abraxas, the numerical value of whose letters is 365. The same name was also employed to denote the Providence which directs the universe, i. e., God in so far he is *manifested*, or the collective hierarchy of emanations. The angels of the lowest heaven (which is that which is seen from earth) created the world and all its inhabitants. The chief angel of this order, called Archon (*ruler*) chose the Jewish nation for *his* subjects, gave them a law by Moses, and designed to make all other people subject to him. But the supreme God sent his Son to hinder this injustice, which Son appeared in the shape of a man; yet his body was a phantom, which at the crucifixion was transferred to Simon the Cyrenian, who suffered in his stead on the cross. He held that the souls which obey the precepts of the Son of God will ascend to God; the punishment of others is a transmigration, according to the doctrines of Pythagoras, whom he followed in several particulars. The moral system of Basilides is said to have allowed nearly every species of iniquity; but there is good evidence that he himself recommended purity of life.

HADRIAN.—FOURTH GENERAL PERSECUTION.

Trajan died in the year 117, and was succeeded by his nephew Ælius Hadrianus, a Prince of admirable accomplishments, yet proud, envious, and revengeful. He rebuilt Jerusalem 62 years after its destruction by Titus, and called it Ælia Capitolina. He also erected a temple to Jupiter Capitolinus, on the site of Solomon's Temple. This and other insults so aggravated the Jews, that in the year 132 they broke out into open rebellion; their leader was Bar-Cocab, who gave himself out as the very star foretold by Balaam (Numb. 24. 17), and committed great outrages upon the Christians, because they would not join his standard and acknowledge him as the expected Messiah. The Romans, probably, learned from this to distinguish more accurately than they had heretofore done between Jews and Christians. This impostor acted more like a robber than a king; but his followers increased so much that a fierce and bloody contest was maintained against the power of Rome for nearly four years. At length Bitthera, a strong place not far from Jerusalem, whither vast numbers of Jews had retired as to a last refuge, fell before Julius Severus in 235, and the revolt was suppressed after terrific slaughter. This was the last and most dreadful dispersion of the Jews; they were forbidden to come within view of Jerusalem, except for one hour on the anniversary of the day on which it was taken by Titus (August 10).

APOLOGIES OF QUADRATUS AND ARISTIDES.

Hadrian passed several years in travel, in the course of which he paid more than one visit to Athens. Having lost its Bishop, Publius, under Trajan's persecution, the Church at this place fell into a low condition, for want of a head. But

Quadratus being constituted Bishop retrieved the ancient spirit of religion. A heavy persecution was raging when Hadrian was in the city, about the year 125, which induced Quadratus to present an Apology or defence to the Emperor in writing, vindicating Christianity from the calumnies of its enemies, and explaining its true character to the heathen. About the same time, Aristides, a Christian philosopher of Athens, presented another apology to Hadrian; but neither this nor that of Quadratus has come down to us.

HADRIAN'S DECREE.

The law of Trajan was a great restraint to the enemies of the Christians, because few persons were willing to assume the dangerous office of accusers. But at the seasons of the public games, when the people were allowed to ask what they pleased of the Emperor or Magistrate, they excited the populace to demand the destruction of the Christians, as wretches whose impiety was the cause of floods and earthquakes; of plagues, famines, and defeats; and these clamors could hardly be disregarded without risk of an insurrection. In the year 126, Serenius Granianus, Proconsul of Asia, represented to the Emperor the injustice of immolating men convicted of no crime, at the pleasure of a furious mob. In consequence of this representation, reaching him close upon the Apologies of Quadratus and Aristides, Hadrian addressed a decree to Minucius Fundanus, and other presidents of provinces, forbidding the Christians to be put to death, unless accused in due form and convicted of having committed some real violation of the laws; and ordering that if the charge were only calumny, the author of it should be punished "according to the heinousness of so mischievous a design." This decree was more favorable to the Christians than that of Trajan, inasmuch as the latter made perseverance in the profession of Christianity a capital offence, whereas the former required violation of the laws before the infliction of punishment, and provided a penalty for false accusers.

ANTONINUS PIUS.

Hadrian died at Baiæ, A. D. 138, and was succeeded by Antoninus (afterwards surnamed Pius, on account of his many virtues), whom Hadrian had adopted a short time before. Under his government it is most probable that the Christians enjoyed considerable repose; and as to the Jews, he relaxed the severity of two edicts of Hadrian, which forbade them to practice circumcision as a distinctive mark of nationality. Yet the heathen, who generally ascribed public calamities to the Christians, did not want pretences for afflicting them, so that this reign was not without martyrs. We read in particular that Telesphorus, seventh Bishop of Rome, suffered in the first year of Antoninus, and if one so eminent fell, we may infer that others of less note shared the same fate. It is supposed by some that Telesphorus was the first Bishop of Rome who met with a violent death, because Irenæus mentions them all in order, yet does not advert to the martyrdom of any before Teleshorus.

VALENTINUS.

The Valentinian heresy holds the most distinguished rank among those which prevailed in the second century. Its founder, Valentinus, an Egyptian, said by Tertullian to have been disappointed of a bishopric, quitted his faith and his country, and taught his doctrines at Rome, about the year 142, whence they were diffused through Europe, Africa, and Asia.

His heresy was a branch of Gnosticism. Refining upon the established genealogies of the Œons, he arranged and named them according to his own inventive imagination, making the number of them thirty, fifteen male and fifteen female, by whose united agency Jesus was mysteriously produced. He held that Jesus Christ's bodily appearance descended with Him from Heaven, and that He received nothing corporeal from His mother; denied the resurrection; and believed in the transmigration of souls. The Valentinian system was plausible in the eyes of Christians, inasmuch as it not only used a Scriptural terminology, but professed to receive all the books of the Scripture, while it was able to set their meaning aside by the most violent misinterpretations. The Gospel of St. John was regarded by the sect as the highest in authority.

CERDON AND MARCION.

About the time that Valentinus broached his heresy, Cerdon and Marcion erected on the foundation of the Gnostics a structure of considerable extent, and taught their doctrines jointly at Rome. Cerdon was a native of Syria, and probably a follower of Saturninus, who taught at Antioch. Marcion is reputed to have been the son of the Bishop of Sinope, in **Pontus**, excommunicated according to Epiphanius, by his father on account of gross immorality.

To the two principles already admitted by the Gnostics, one good and the other evil, they added an intermediate deity, whom they conceived to be the creator of the world and the God of the Jews, and asserted that he was in a state of continual hostility with the evil principle, but desirous of usurping the place of the Supreme Being. Mankind, they asserted, was governed despotically by the two former of these beings; but they added that the Supreme had sent down his own Son, clothed with a shadowy resemblance of a body, for the deliverance of all who, by self-denial and austerity, sought to obtain that happiness. The followers of Cerdon and Marcion were distinguished by the name of the latter. They entirely rejected the Old Testament, and though they admitted some books of the New, for instance the Gospel of St. Luke and ten Epistles of St. Paul, it was not without considerable alterations and mutilations. Marcion is said by Tertullian to have written a book called *Antitheses*, with the view of showing an essential difference between the Old and New Testament.

JUSTIN MARTYR.

Justin Martyr, one of the most eminent persons whose pens were engaged in the cause of Christianity in its early days, was born of Gentile parents at Flavia Neapolis, the ancient Sychem or Shechem, in Samaria, in the year 103. After wandering in pursuit of truth through every known philosophical system, and being greatly moved by the constancy with which Christians endured persecution and death for the sake of their faith, he at length embraced Christianity in the reign of Hadrian (A. D. 133), and without laying aside his philosopher's habit, taught the doctrines of the Gospel at Rome. Here he had frequent contests with Crescens, a noted Cynic philosopher, at whose instigation, it is supposed, he was beheaded at Rome, about the year 165.

NOTE.—The Christians were suffering greatly from the Pagans about the year 148; whereupon Justin wrote his *First Apology*, which he addressed to the Emperor, his adopted sons (M. Aurelius and L. Verus), the Senate, and the people of Rome. In it he vindicates the Christians from the charges of Atheism, immorality, political disaffection, sedition, &c.; and shows the injustice of proceeding against them without form of law. He appeals to the purity of the New Testament morality, to the lives of the Christians, their love even for their enemies, their firmness in confessing the faith, and their patience in suffering for it. He dwells on the chief points of Christian doctrine (among these, the Trinity, the Incarnation, and Eternal life), vindicates the character and miracles of our Lord; and argues from the progress that the Gospel had already made. Subsequently Justin visited the East, and at Ephesus held a disputation for two days with a learned Jew named Trypho, an account of which he has given us in his *Dialogue with Trypho the Jew*. He proves by the Old Testament that Jesus Christ was the Messiah. Justin's *Second Apology* was presented either to Antoninus Pius, or to Marcus Aurelius, most likely to the latter, between the years 161 and 165; he addresses it to the Roman Senate, and remonstrates against the cruelty of putting persons to death merely for the name of Christians, without even accusing them of crime. His voluminous writings are especially valuable, in affording evidence of the truth of the canon of Scripture.

EDICT OF ANTONINUS PIUS.

Justin's first Apology is presumed to have had some effect upon the mind of the Emperor, for soon after its presentation he wrote to different cities of Greece in favor of the Christians. Moreover, about the year 152 either he or his sucessor issued an edict to the cities of Asia Minor, in which he denounced capital punishment against the accusers of the Christians, if they could not convict them of some *crime*. This decree was issued in consequence of outrages committed upon the Christians by the populace, who regarded them as the cause of earthquakes which visited the earth at that time.

NOTE.—In the reign of Antoninus Pius, and while Anicetus was Bishop of Rome, a controversy arose between the Eastern and Western Churches, concerning the time of the celebration of Easter, the festival in commemoration of our Lord's resurrection. Both fasted during "the great week" in which Christ died, and in remembrance of his last supper ate a paschal lamb, just as the Jews did at their Passover. Now, the Eastern or Asiatic Christians, upon the alleged authority of John and Philip, held their paschal feast after the manner of the Jews, on the night of the 14th day of the first Jewish month (Nisan, or March), commemorating the crucifixion on the following day; and on the third day after, whether it fell upon Sunday or not, they commemorated the resurrection of Christ. But the Western Churches, citing Paul and Peter as authors of their custom, put off their paschal feast until the evening preceding the festal day sacred to Christ's resurrection, which was the Sunday next after the full moon of Nisan; and in commemoration of the crucifixion, they set apart good Friday three days before. The Asiatic custom gave much offence to the Western Churches, who regarded it as indecent to interrupt the fas of "the great week," and to commemorate the ressurection on any other day of the week than that on which it actually took place. Great inconvenience was likewise felt when an inhabitant of one country visited another where a different practice prevailed, for one was feasting and rejoicing while another was fasting. Considerable disturbance arose in the Church from this difference with regard to Easter; and with the view of arranging it, Polycarp, Bishop of Smyrna, in the year 158, came all the way to Rome to have a conference with Anicetus, Bishop of Rome, on the subject. Their conference did not end the controversy, but, having first taken the sacrament together, they parted upon friendly terms, and each party adhered to its own custom. Towards the end of the century, Victor, then Bishop of Rome, demanded from the Eastern Churches a compliance with the ritual of the West; and upon their resolute opposition, which was headed by Polycrates, Bishop of Ephesus, he excommunicated the Churches of Asia Minor from all communion with his own. And though the censure was withdrawn on the strong remonstrance of Irenæus, Bishop of Lyons, and the Asiatic prelates, yet the schism was not finally healed until the Council of Nice, in 325, which abolished the Eastern custom and confirmed that of the West.

MARCUS AURELIUS.—FIFTH GENERAL PERSECUTION.

Marcus Aurelius, the celebrated Stoic Philosopher, succeeded to empire in the year 161. He was a prince of admirable virtues and accomplishments, alloyed with much Pagan superstition. He appears to have been solicited to persecute the Christians in order to appease the heathen deities, and prevent the recurrence of pestilence and earthquakes, which were attributed to the toleration of Christians. He declined, and issued an edict similar to that of his predecessor, requiring that the commission of some crime must be proved against any one before he could be punished, and denouncing capital punishment against the accuser of a Christian as such. Notwithstanding this edict, persecution prevailed extensively during the greater part of his reign, connived at, and probably encouraged, by this most philosophic of the Roman emperors. Lardner assigns three reasons for this: — (1) The Christians refused to join in the common worship of the heathen deities, and reflected freely upon the Philosophers; (2) They out-did the Stoics in patience under suffering; (3) The emperor was a bigot in religion and philosophy.

MARTYRDOM OF POLYCARP.

Polycarp had been a disciple of John the Apostle, and was nearly ninety years old. Every effort was made to make him renounce his faith. While in the amphitheater, expecting execution, the pro-consul Quadratus said, "Swear, and I will release thee — reproach Christ!" But Polycarp replied, "Eighty and six years do I serve him, and never hath he injured me; and how can I blaspheme my King and Saviour?" "I have wild beasts," said the persecutor. "Call them," replied the hero, "I cannot change from good to evil; it is good to change from sin to righteousness." "I will cause thee to be devoured by fire," continued Quadratus, "since thou despisest the beasts." Polycarp responded, "Thou threatenest the fire which burneth but for a time and is then extinguished, for thou knowest not the fire of future judgment and of eternal punishment reserved for the wicked. But why tarriest thou? Bring what thou wilt!" He died in the midst of the flames, thanking God for the honor of sealing his faith by his blood.

MONTANUS AND HIS SCHISM.

In the reign of Marcus Aurelius arose an illiterate sect, opposed to all learning and philosphy. They took their name from Montanus, an obscure men of weak judgment, who, about the year 168, became notorious at Pepuza, a village of Mysia, on the confines of Phrygia, whence they were sometimes called *Pepuzians, Phrygians,* or *Cataphrygians.*

Montanus was a wild enthusiast, who pretended to an extraordinary degree of inspiration, and affirmed himself to be the *Paraclete*, or Comforter promised by Christ; and that he was sent to perfect the moral doctrines of Christ. He made a distinction between the Comforter promised by Christ to his Apostles, and the Holy Spirit which was shed upon them on the day of Pentecost, and considered the former as a Divine teacher, which character he himself assumed. Averse to the arts which improve and the enjoyments which embellish human life, Montanus and his followers anathematized learning and philosophy, and were distinguished by extreme austerity: they held the heavier sins, as apostasy, murder, and adultery, to be irremissible, and maintained that Christians sinned grievously who saved their lives by flight in the time of persecution. It does not appear that Montanus was heretical in the fundamental articles of our faith; but on account of his practices he was excluded from connection with the Church. The severity of his discipline led some persons of no mean condition to put faith in him, especially two ladies of quality—Priscilla and Maximilla, who left their husbands to preach in public, according to the dictates of their prophetic Spirit, which was generally exerted in denuncitions of woe to the world, particularly to the Roman empire. Of all his followers, the most distinguished was the learned and austere Tertullian.

BARDISANES AND HIS HERESY.

Bardisanes, a native of Edessa, in Mesopotamia, a man of great acumen, and distinguished for many learned productions, one of which was directed against the heretic Marcion, flourished also in this reign. Apollonius, a Stoic philosopher, endeavored in every possible way to induce him to renounce Christianity; and his efforts, though baffled for a while, were at last partially succesful. Seduced by his attachment to the oriental philosophy, he became infected with Gnostic errors, holding the doctrine of two principles, and with Valentinus denying the resurrection of the dead, and believing that Jesus was a phantom. He acknowledged, indeed, the Law and the Prophets, together with the New Testament, but admitted several Apocryphal books along with them. He is said to have abjured some of his errors before he died; and was never considered so decidedly heretical as many others of the Gnostics. His followers, however, added new errors to his own, and were celled *Bardesanites*.

PERSECUTION AT LYONS AND VIENNE.

Towards the close of the second century, Christianity was making great progress in the south of France, whither Polycarp, Bishop of Smyrna, is supposed to have sent missionaries. In the year 177, a most bloody persecution arose at Lyons and Vienne, in Gaul. The brutal cruelty of the Pagans exceeded all that had been experienced before, as we learn from a letter sent by the Christians of those cities to the Churches of Asia and Phrygia, and preserved by Eusebius. The Christians were hunted from their houses, forbidden to shew their heads, dragged from place to place, plundered, stoned, cast into prison, and there treated with all the marks of ungovernable fury; their slaves, too, were tortured to charge their masters with abominable crimes in private. Numbers who confessed themselves Christians, after undergoing exquisite torments, were put to death, and their mangled remains thrown into the Rhone: and a few who denied their faith, upon witnessing the steadfastness of their brethren, recovered their firmness and suffered like the rest. One Attalus endured great torture; but the Governor, upon learning that he was a Roman citizen, became afraid of committing himself with a privileged person, and wrote to know the Emperor's pleasure. Aurelius answered that "those who confessed themselves Christians should suffer, whether they were Roman citizens or not; but those who renounced the faith should be dismissed." Neither age nor sex was spared: Pothinus, Bishop of Lyons, a venerable person of 90 years of age, after being scourged by the officers; kicked, beaten, and pelted by the crowd; was carried almost lifeless to a prison, where he died within two days. An admirable woman named Blandina, and a boy named Ponticus, were among the most distinguished sufferers, and the malice of the heathen did not end with the death of their victims. They cast their bodies to the dogs; they burnt such fragments as were left uneaten, and threw the ashes into the Rhone, in mockery of the doctrine of a resurrection.

IRENÆUS.

During the persecution at Lyons, Irenæus, a Presbyter of the Church there, was despatched to Rome with a letter to Eleutherus, the Bishop of that See, touching his Montanism. To his absence on this mission Irenæus probably owed his life. He was a native of Asia Minor, and a pupil of Polycarp. After his return from Rome he was made Bishop of Lyons, in the room of the martyr Ponthinus, in which position he acted with so much wisdom and zeal that, according to Gregory of Tours, he made almost all the city Christians. He died, probably by martyrdom, in the year 202.

CHRISTIANITY IN BRITAIN.

There is a tradition that in the latter part of the second century, probably about the year 178, Lucius, a king or chieftain of Britain, applied to Eleutherus, Bishop of Rome, for assistance with regard to instruction in religion, and that two eminent men were consequently sent over from Rome, by whose means Christianity was widely diffused in that island. Hence Lucius has been called the first Christian king.

COMMODUS.

The Emperor Marcus Aurelius having died in the year 180, his son Commodus, then in his 19th year, was acknowledged as his successor. During the reign of Commodus, the Christians were in a great measure eased from persecution, in consequence partly of the emperor's indifference to all matters connected with religion, and partly, it is presumed, of the protection shown to them by Marcia, the emperor's favorite mistress, who, notwithstanding her present abandoned life, had once professed Christianity. The consequence of this repose was that the new religion travelled into distant countries, which had scarcely yet submitted to the Roman arms. It was also embraced by persons of rank, as is shown in the case of Apollonius, the only distinguished martyr in this reign. Apollonius was a Roman Senator, who, upon being accused of professing Christianity by his own servant, made a learned and eloquent apology for the Christian religion before the Senate. He was ordered to be executed, and a similar fate was awarded to his accuser, under the law of Antoninus Pius.

SEVERUS.

Commodus died at the latter end of the year 192. He was succeeded by Pertinax and Julianus, whose reigns endured less than half a year. Upon the death of the latter, Septimius Severus, Niger, and Albinus put forth their claims to the imperial diadem, the first of whom was proclaimed sole emperor in the year 193. His temper and circumstances disposed him to the performance both of the noblest acts and bloodiest severities.

HERESY OF THEODOTUS AND ARTEMON.

In the earliest part of the reign of Severus the Church began to be infected with two different forms of heresy. The difficulty of reconciling the doctrine of the Divine Unity with that of the Trinity induced some (as Theodotus, Artemon, &c.,) to deny the Godhead of the Second and Third persons; and others (as Praxeas, Nœtus, Sabellius, &c.,) to look upon the three Persons as merely denoting three different manifestations of the same Divine Person.

Theodotus, a tanner, of Byzantium, who, in the time of persecution, during the siege of the city by Severus, had from fear of torture denied Jesus Christ, to vindicate his apostasy afterwards at Rome, added that he had not denied God, but man, which was tantamount to asserting the simple humanity of Jesus Christ. Hence, Theodotus is regarded as the founder of the heresy which denies the Divinity of our Saviour : for, although some the Gnostics maintained that Jesus was a mere man, and Christ an emanation which descended upon Him from heaven at His baptism, they did not affirm the humanity of Jesus Christ. Like the first Socinians, Theodotus taught that Christ was miraculously conceived, and born of a virgin. He was excommunicated by Victor, Bishop of Rome. A celebrated disciple of his was Arteman, or Artemas. Natalius, too, adopted his views, and "was persuaded," says Eusebius, "to be created a Bishop of this heresy; with a salary of 120 denarii a month" (about $300 a year). The salary of Natalius was probably not a correct gauge of that which was the usual stipend of the corresponding functionary of the Church, as heretics were then an inconsiderable body, and could not afford a large payment to their leader. Natalius lived to abjure his errors.

THE PATRIPASSIANS.

Soon after the Theodotian heresy was broached, one Praxeas, a person of Asia Minor, who had been a Montanist, and was imprisoned for the cause of Christ, promulgated a grievous heresy upon the subject of the Trinity.

Discarding all real distinction between the Father, Son, and Holy Ghost, he maintained that the two latter were only modes or operations of the one Being called God. Hence his followers were called *Monarchians*, because of their denying the plurality of persons in the Deity, and *Patripassians* (*Pater, father*, and *Pascho, to suffer*), because, as Tertullian shows, their doctrine leads to the belief that the Father was so intimately united with the Son, that He himself suffered the anguish of an afflicted life and the torments of an ignominious death. Their doctrine resembled those of the modern Unitarians. It does not appear that this sect separated from the ordinary assemblies of Christians. Nœtus, Beryllus, Sabellius, and Paul of Samosata supported this heresy; and Tertullian, Hippolytus, Origin, and Dionysius of Alexandria opposed it.

TERTULLIAN.

NOTE. — Towards the end of the second century appeared that celebrated Christian author, Tertullian. He was born at Carthage, and educated there in the Pagan religion, which, however, he forsook in the beginning of the reign of Severus, and was made a Presbyter of the Church, and in that character resided both at Carthage and at Rome. In his writings he showed himself a rigid censor and nice asserter of the severities of religion; until at length disgusted with some affronts he met with at Rome, and incited by his own vehement and austere disposition, he embraced the errors of Montanus, about the year 200, and continued in them until his death about the year 218 or 220. Tertullian was. perhaps the most eminent man that had arisen since the days of the Apostles. From the style of his writings, as well as from his acquaintance with law and forensic terms, it seems probable that he had followed the profession of an advocate. He was master of the Greek language to such a degree as to be able to write treatises in it. If not the very first of the Latin Fathers (for Minucius Felix is said to have been his senior), yet to him we are indebted for the earliest specimen of ecclesiastical Latin. Hitherto, the language of the Western Churches, not only in the Greek colonies of Gaul, but at Rome itself, had been Greek — the general medium of communication, and the tongue in which the oracles of Christianity were written. His works were very voluminous; the most famous of them was his *Apology for the Christians against the Heathen*, addressed to the magistrates and governors of the Roman empire. In this work he complains of the unjust and illegal proceedings against the Christians; demonstrates the falsehood of the charges of crime brought against them; shows their temperance, piety, obedience, soundness of principle, and the unreasonableness of laying national calamities at their doors; and asserts the superiority of Christian virtues over those of the Pagan philosophers.

THE THIRD CENTURY.

SIXTH GENERAL PERSECUTION.

The early part of the reign of Severus was so favorable to the Christians, that no additions were made to the severe edicts in force against them. Probably they were indebted for this lenity to Proculus, a Christian, who cured the emperor of a dangerous distemper. But this precarious peace, interrupted by the partial execution of severe laws, was terminated in the year 202, by an edict more intolerant than any which had preceded it. This edict prohibited every subject of the empire, under the penalties of death and confiscation of property, from embracing the Jewish or Christian faith. The persecution raged violently for seven years, in various parts of the empire. Irenæus, Bishop of Lyons, and Victor, Bishop of Rome, were among the most celebrated martyrs. But nowhere was the persecution felt more bitterly than at Alexandria, which was visited by the emperor about this time. Among the sufferers were Leonidas, father of the renowed Origen; and Potamiena, a woman not less distinguished for chastity than for beauty, who, with her mother, Marcella, was burned to death, boiling pitch being poured over their naked bodies. These calamities induced Tertullian to compose his *Apology* and some other works.

ORIGEN.

NOTE. — *His Life and Writings.* The industry, erudition, and accomplishments of Origen justly entitle him to the most distinguished place amongst the Christian writers of the third century. He was born in the year 185, of Christian parents, in Egypt, and his education, commenced under a learned and devout father, was completed under Clemens Alexandrinus and the philosopher Ammonius Saccas. When his father Leonidas suffered martyrdom under Severus, the urgent entreaties of his mother, who is said to have been obliged to hide his clothes, were barely sufficient to prevent her son, then only a youth of seventeen, from suffering in the same cause. He wrote, however, to his father in prison, exhorting him to steadfastness in the faith, although the support of his wife and seven children depended upon his life. The property of the family having been confiscated, Origen supported them for a short time by teaching; but upon the retirement of Clemens in 203, although only 18 years old, he was advanced, by Demetrius, the Bishop of Alexandria, to the mastership of the Catechetical school there, the reputation of which he greatly extended. In the year 213 he paid a short visit to Rome, when the church was then under the government of Zephyrinus, and upon his return to Alexandria he associated his former pupil Heraclas, eventually Bishop of Alexandria, with him in the school, so that he had more time to devote to theology and the exposition of the Scriptures. Being compelled in 215 by the persecution under Caracalla, son of Severus, to flee from Alexandria, he retired to Cæsarea in Palestine, where, upon the occasion of a subsequent visit about 228, he was ordained presbyter by Theoctistus, Bishop of Cæsarea, and Alexander, Bishop of Jerusalem. Demetrius, Bishop of Alexandria, complained of the irregularity of foreign Bishops ordaining *his* laymen, which complaint was met by the plea that Demetrius himself had furnished Origen with a commendatory letter. Controversy ensued, and in the year 230 Demetrius assembled two councils against Origen, by which he was deprived of his office in the Catechetical school, his orders were annulled, and he was excommunicated as a heretic; and it does not appear that any attempt was ever made by Heraclas, the successor of Demetrius, to rescind the condemnation of his former teacher and colleague. He now settled at Cæsarea in Palestine for a time, but was driven from it to Cæsarea in Cappadocia by the persecution under Maximinus, in 235. Upon the death of Maximinus he returned to Palestine. In the Decian persecution he endured imprisonment and torture; and he died at length at Tyre, in the 69th year of his age, A. D. 253.

PERSECUTION AT ROME.

The persecuting edict of Severus was issued during the emperor's absence from Rome; but he sent to the capital an order for bringing before the prefect all persons attending illegal meetings, under which term Christian assemblies were made to rank. In 203 the emperor returned to Rome, and celebrated a triumph with great magnificence for his successes over the nations he had subdued in his recent expeditions. In the following year he chose to celebrate the Secular games out of their regular course. These spectacles and solemnities were attended with their usual consequences to the Christians, who were unwilling to join in them, and there is but little doubt that the cruelty exercised against them was terrible. Zephyrinus was Bishop of Rome at this time.

RAPID SUCCESSION OF ROMAN EMPERORS.

The Emperor Severus died at York A. D. 211, after a residence of two years in Britain. He was suceeded by his son Caracalla, who was slain in 217, after a barbarous reign of six years. Macrinus succeeded to the imperial purple, but was slain in 218; whereupon Elagabalus obtained the vacant eminence, and he too was slain in the year 222, after a reign of less than four years. This quick succession of Roman Emperors was favorable to the diffusion of Christianity. The events attending their lives and deaths and the artifices of candidates for the diadem naturally engaged much public attention, and suspended the execution of those sanguinary edicts intended for the destruction of the Christians.

ALEXANDER SEVERUS.

Upon the death of Elagabalus in 222, Alexander Severus was acknowledged emperor. He was an excellent and virtuous prince. The laws against the Christians were not repealed by him, so that in his vast empire instances occur of Christians suffering death in his reign; yet from the influence of his mother, Mammæa, who had been instructed by Origen, he showed kind feelings towards them in various ways, and was indeed the first Roman Emperor by whom they were expressly tolerated. It is said that he had an image of Christ in his chamber, where he performed his daily devotions; but, as a blind man without full knowledge, he placed Christ with Orpheus, Apollonius of Tyana, and his other deities. He adopted the custom of the Christians in their ecclesiastical appointments, by publishing the names of intended governors of provinces and cities, and inviting objections against their fitness. Moreover, he inscribed upon his palace and public buildings the Christian command, "*Quod tibi fieri non vis, alteri ne feceris,*" *Do not that to another, which you would not have another do to you,* and once designed to erect a temple to Jesus Christ. In addition to these evidences of a favorable feeling towards Christianity, he adjudged a piece of ground in dispute between some tavern-keepers and the Christians to the latter, saying, "it is better that God be there worshiped in any manner, than that the place should be put to such uses as they (the tavern-keepers) designed it for." Supposing that there was some building upon the spot of ground, we have here the oldest testimony of any edifice publicly consecrated to the worship of our holy religion, known to be such by the Pagans. The early Christians, as we have seen, were accustomed to meet for worship in each other's houses.

COUNCIL OF ICONIUM.

In this reign, probably about the year 231, the Council of Iconium was called to determine a controversy concerning the validity of the baptism administered by the Montanists. Familianus, and fifty Bishops from Phrygia, Galatia, Cilicia, and Cappadocia, were present. It was resolved that all baptism administered out of the Church was to be rejected, as had been done before in Cappadocia by immemorial custom. Before this time, the Montanists, who were not at first schismatics, appear to have refused to join in communion with the other members of the Church. They formed themselves into separate communities, adhering, however, to the outward form of ecclesiastical government which had now been established two centuries. It was the admission of members into the Church by the sacrament of Baptism used by them which led to the decisive step against them by the Council of Iconium.

MAXIMINUS.—SEVENTH GENERAL PERSECUTION.

Alexander Severus was slain by his soldiers in his tent, in a campaign against the Germans, in the year 235, and was succeeded by Maximinus, an old soldier, who was instrumental in his death. He was a giant in stature, and of a most cruel temper. No sooner was he secure in his high station than he put to death all such as had been intimate with Alexander, and banished those who had been advanced by him. In the midst of so much cruelty and bloodshed, no wonder that the savage included the Christians in his persecution; yet the severities they endured were probably to be ascribed more to his displeasure at their uttachment to the former emperor, and their having been protected by him, than to their religious principles. The persecution in his reign was directed chiefly against the bishops and ministers of the Church, as the pillars and propagators of Christianity. Maximinus was slain after a reign of three years; and his successors Maximus and Balbinus, who reigned jointly, shared the same fate soon after.

GORDIAN.

Gordian succeeded to the empire in the year 238, at the age of fourteen. He was a youth of excellent disposition; and during his reign the Church enjoyed tranquility, and Christians used to meet in large assemblies to settle their own affairs without molestation. We have a record of ninety Bishops having met in council at Carthage, upon the heresy of one Privatus, which shows that the Gospel had at that time made very great advance in Africa.

HERESY OF BERYLLUS.

In the reign of Gordian, about the year 242, the Church in Arabia was disturbed by Beryllus, Bishop of Bostra.

He asserted that in the unity of the Godhead there is no distinction of Persons — that our Saviour before His Incarnation had no proper subsistence, no personal deity, but only a derivative divinity from the Father afterwards. Praxeas and Nœtus had already disseminated similar errors, and they were subsequently modified and brought into greater notice by Sabellius. The Bishops of Arabia met, and condemned the doctrine, but could not convince Beryllus of his errors; whereupon they requested the assistance of Origen, by whom he was so lucidly confuted that he returned into the bosom of the Church.

PHILIP.

Gordian was succeeded by Philip, an Arabian of dishonorable parentage, in the year 244. Notwithstanding many unjustifiable actions, he has been held to have been a Christian, and consequently the first Christian emperor of Rome. That this opinion is fallacious is highly probable; but this much may be deduced from it, that the clemency of the emperor was favorable to Christianity, and that the doctrines of the Gospel were embraced by many, whom the dread of a persecuting tyrant would have prevented from making an open profession of their faith in Christ. The only disturbance during this reign was occasioned by a popular outbreak at Alexandria, in which many lives were lost.

CYPRIAN.

NOTE.—In the year 246, the famous Cyprian, a teacher of rhetoric at Carthage, was converted to Christianity, in the 46th year of his age. He was rapidly promoted to the offices of deacon and presbyter; and with the exception of Novatus, who afterwards fled to Rome for fear of being excommunicated, and four other dissentient presbyters, he was unanimously made Bishop of Carthage in 248. In the Decian persecution, A. D. 250, he withdrew to a retreat at no great distance, contriving during his exile to regulate the affairs of his Church, to which he returned at the close of the persecution. He then entered into a spirited controversy with Stephen, Bishop of Rome, concerning the re-baptizing of converted heretics. At Rome the custom had been to admit proselytes by imposition of hands. In Asia and Africa re-baptism had been practised on the principle that baptism by heretics was null. Cyprian, therefore, contended, in opposition to the arrogant Stephen, that re-baptism was necessary on the admission of converts from heresy and schism into the Church. The severe edicts of Valerian were fatal to Cyprian. He was first banished to Curubis, about fifty miles from Carthage, and in the following year recalled to Carthage, where he was confined to the narrow limits of his own garden. Refusing to purchase life by sacrificing to the gods, he was beheaded in the year 258. Naturally ardent, and attached to the works of Tertullian, he imbibed much of the spirit of that gloomy Montanist; and having high ideas of episcopal power and great intrepidity of character, he was an energetic prelate and severe disciplinarian. His works, which are nearly all practical, consist of 81 Epistles and 14 Treatises. The Novatian schism took place during his Episcopate. Among the chief controversies in which he was engaged were those upon the subject of the lapsed, baptism by heretics, and Novatianism.

DECIUS.—EIGHTH GENERAL PERSECUTION.

Philip fell in a mutiny of soldiers, in the year 249, and was succeeded by Decius Trajan. For forty years the Church had enjoyed comparative tranquility and made proportionate advances: but prosperity had produced not unusual effects by introducing various corruptions and growing laxity of discipline. The reign of Decius brought with it a fiery 'trial of Christianity, which Cyprian regarded as a chastisement from Heaven for the corruptions which had grown up with the Church's security. Eusebius ascribes this fearful persecution to the hatred of Decius for his predecessor Philip, whom he accounted a Christian; others attributed it to the triumphant increase of Christianity, and the consequent declension of paganism. Decius, it is said, was so enraged to see the religion of the empire trodden under foot, and undermined by a novel sect, that he issued edicts to the governors of provinces, commanding them to proceed against the Christians with the utmost severity, and to spare no kind of torments, and to put to death all who refused to sacrifice to the gods. Nothing can be imagined more dismal than the storm which followed in all parts of the empire; the heart sickens at the recital of the ingenious and diversified tortures to which the Christians were exposed. Some apostatized, but the greater part remained unshaken. The persecution was especially directed against the bishops and the clergy. Fabion, Bishop of Rome, was put to death; the Bishops of Alexandria, Carthage, and Neocæsarea, (viz., Dionysius, Cyprian, and Gregory), were obliged to conceal themselves for a time. Alexander, Bishop of Jerusalem, and Babylas, Bishop of Antioch, died in prison; Origen also underwent many cruel tortures. Eudæmon, of Smyrna, is the only bishop related to have renounced his faith. "There was general confusion and consternation," says an old writer, "the laws of nature and humanity were trodden under foot; friend betrayed his friend, brother his brother, and children their parents, every man being afraid of his nearest relations. By this means the woods and mountains became full; the cities and towns empty."

MONACHISM.

Hence arose monks and hermits. The prevalence of Platonic Christianity, and the belief that solitude, contemplation, and abstinence were necessary to elevate the soul to a knowledge of Divine Truth, had already prepared the way for Monachism, which assumed a definite form in the Decian persecution, during which Paul of Thebes, the first Christian hermit, fled into the Egyptian deserts, and led there a solitary life for ninety years. His example was followed by many others, and a voluntary seclusion from secular affairs came to be inculcated as the perfection of piety and virtue.

CHAPTER III.

From the Rise of Monachism till the Council at Nice.
A. D. 249-325.

I. THE THIRD CENTURY.—Continued.

GALLUS.

Decius perished in an attack upon the Goths, A. D. 251, and was succeeded in the empire by Gallus, who in a short time after his succession renewed the persecution against the Christians, which had considerably abated. Without issuing new decrees, he enforced the former ones, compelling the Christians, to sacrifice. A pestilence then raging in the empire contributed to influence the persecution, for visitations of this sort were charged upon the lenity shown to the Christians. Cyprian vindicated Christianity from this vulgar and popular objection, in a treatise addressed to Demetrian, the Proconsul of Carthage. In this persecution Cornelius, Bishop of Rome, was first banished to Civitia Vecchia, and then beheaded; and his successor Lucius suffered a like fate.

VALERIAN.—NINTH GENERAL PERSECUTION.

After a short reign, Gallus was slain, A. D. 253. Æmilian, who succeeded him, held the empire only four months. He was succeeded by Valerian, who began his reign with many kindnesses towards the Christians, entertaining them even in his own family. But after about four years of peace, a most bitter persecution broke out. In the year 257, Valerian, at the instigation of his prime minister, Macrianus, who charged the Christians with hindering by wicked charms the prosperity of the empire, issued an edict, commanding all persons to adopt the religious ceremonies of Rome, prohibiting the Christians from holding meetings, and ordering Bishops and other teachers into exile. The martyrs in this persecution were innumerable; among the chief of them was Stephen (successor of Lucius), Bishop of Rome, who was succeeded by Xystus; Cyprian also,

Bishop of Carthage, was banished, and subsequently put to death. Next year, 258, Valerian published a still more severe edict; wherein he ordered that Bishops, Presbyters, and Deacons should be put to death without delay; that senators and persons of rank should forfeit their honor and estates, and their lives also, if they persisted in Christianity; that ladies lose property and be sent into banishment; and that the imperial household should be imprisoned. At Rome, Xystus, the bishop, and Laurenitnus, a deacon, were roasted before a slow fire; and in all the provinces numbers of Christians were put to death, or exposed to sufferings worse than death. After the death of Xystus, the Church at Rome continued for nearly a year without a bishop; but upon the persecution somewhat abating, Dionysius was appointed to that office.

INFANT BAPTISM.

The peace which the Church enjoyed in the early part of Valerian's reign gave opportunity to the Bishops to make several regulations. Amongst others, a council was called at Carthage, by Cyprian, concerning the time of baptizing infants, a question started by Fidus, an African Bishop, who asserted that baptism was not to be administered until the eighth day, as circumcision was under the Jewish law. The council decided that it was not necessary to defer baptism until the eighth day, nor was the mercy of God to be denied to any as soon as born into the world.

THE SABELLIAN HERESY.

The Sabellians were so called from Sabellius, an African Presbyter or Bishop, at Ptolemais, a district of Pentapolis, who started his heretical notions about A. D. 257.

He taught that there is but *one* person in the Godhead, who manifested himself in three different ways — thus reducing the three persons in the Trinity to three characters or relations, and maintaining that the Word and Holy Spirit are only emanations or functions of the Deity, put forth only for a particular time and purpose. Thus, he compared the Divinity to the Son, of which the Father would be analogous to the substance, the Son to the light, and the Holy Ghost to the heat. This doctrine somewhat differed from that advanced by Praxeas, Nœtus, Beryllus, with which it has sometimes been identified. The former heretics supposed that the Father *personally* assumed the human nature of Christ; whereas Sabellius held that it was only a part of the Divine nature, which was put forth as an emanation and became united with the Son, and the Holy Spirit he considered to be a similar portion of the Supreme Father.

The Sabellian heresy was checked by the opposition of Dionysius, Bishop of Alexandria, and its author was condemned in a council held at Rome in the year 263.

GALLIENUS.

Valerian having been taken prisoner by Sopores, King of Persia (by whom he was subsequently flayed alive), his son Gallienus became emperor, A. D. 260. National calamities attended his advent to power; and recollecting that while his father favored the Christians, Heaven smiled upon his designs, Gallienus by his edicts relaxed the persecution against them, and allowed them a full freedom in the use of their religion. The Bishopric of Rome, which had been vacant for some time, was filled up by the election of Dionysius, a man of considerable learning. Although in consequence of dissensions among its own members, the Church was not wholly without troubles and martyrs, it may be said that from this time it enjoyed a peace of forty years.

PAULIANISTS.

The Paulianists, or Paulians, derived their name from Paul of Samosata, in Syria, who was elected Bishop of Antioch, A. D. 260. His doctrine is described as akin to that of Artemon. He asserted the simple humanity of Christ; but maintained that the Spirit of the Father had descended upon Him, dwelt within Him (but without any personal union), and empowered Him to work miracles and instruct mankind; and that in this sense he is called the Son of God. Ancient writers have accused this first heretical bishop of having sought to present the doctrine concerning Christ in a dress acceptable to Jewish modes of thinking, with a view to gain the favor of Zenobia, queen of Palmyra, who had possession of Antioch, and is said to have been friendly to Judaism. A council to consider his opinions was held at Antioch in 265, and was attended by the Bishops of all the principal Asiatic sees. He so concealed his real sentiments, however, under ambiguous forms of speech that the council, under the advice of Firmilianus, of Cæsarea, separated without any formal decision. But at last, in 269, the Bishop having continued to propagate his heretical doctrines, a second council was held, which began its proceedings by addressing a letter (which is still extant) to Paul, maintaining the essential Divinity of Christ; His eternal pre-existence; His creation of the world; His relation to God as a Son, not as a creature; and His miraculous Incarnation. After a long discussion, in the course of which various questions were put to Paul, and afterwards published, he was deposed and excommunicated, and Domnus, son of his predecessor, appointed in his place; although under the protection of Zenobia he continued to enjoy the emoluments of his episcopal rank for four years. On the defeat of Zenobia, he was rejected by a decree of Aurelian, in the year 272, and Domnus, the Bishop elect, was thus confirmed in his office. The followers of Paul were not very numerous; yet his distinguished rank, his ostentation, his opulence, and his vigorous opposition to the decrees of councils attracted general attention.

GREGORY THAUMATURGUS.

Gregory, Bishop of Neocæsarea in Pontus, surnamed Thaumaturgus, flourished in this reign. His original name was Theodorus; he was born of heathen parents about the year 200, and having become a pupil of Origen at Cæsarea in Palestine was converted about 231. Soon after his ordination in 240 he was appointed Bishop of Neocesarea, where he died in 270, having retired for a short time in the Decean persecution. The miracles ascribed to Gregory have bestowed upon him a degree of celebrity which probably he would not have derived from his few literary productions. The Sabellians claimed him, though unjustly, as a favorer of their views, because in explaining to the heathen that the Father and the Son are one in essence, he seemed to say that they are two only metaphisically, not really. He wrote several epistles, an oration in praise of Origen, a paraphrase on Ecclesiastes, and probably a creed.

AURELIAN.

Claudius, who was proclaimed emperor, when Gallienus was slain in the year 268, reigned little more than two years, when he was succeeded by Aurelian in the year 270. For four years the Christians enjoyed peace. But in the fifth year of his reign,

Aurelian, prompted either by his own superstition, or by that of others, prepared to persecute them. Before his edicts, however, had been published over the whole empire, he was assassinated at Thrace, A. D. 275. At his death an interregnum of six months ensued, and the succeeding emperors were Tacitus, Probus, and Carus, whose reigns were not unfavorable to Christianity.

MANICHÆISM.

Manichæism appeared in Europe in the reign of Probus. Its founder was one Manes, or Manichæis, concerning whose origin various stories exist. He was probably born in Persia about the year 240, and was put to death by the Persian government about 277. His system was a compound of Gnostic, Pythagorian, and Christian doctrines.

He gave himself out as the Paraclete who, according to our Saviour's promise, was to communicate to the world a clearer and fuller revelation; and taught the doctrine of two principles, one of which was a living Light, existing from all eternity, and surrounded by hosts of pure spirits; and the other an evil power called Darkness, who had resided from eternity in a remote region of infinite space, accompanied by myriads of evil spirits created out of matter, of which his kingdom was composed. There was a time when these powers were unaquainted with each other's existence; but the spirits of Darkness, having once advanced beyond their own limits and beheld the delightful realms of light, projected an irruption into his kingdom. To these turbulent spirits God opposed the *first man;* but his opposition being too feeble, the *living spirit* was sent to his aid : a part of the celestial substance, however, being seized by demons, light and darkness became blended. From the parts of this mixture uncontaminated, or contaminated only in a small degree, with matter, the sun, moon, and planets were formed. The remainder composed this world, fitted for the residence of bodies endued with a soul composed of those parts of the celestial substance which the prince of Darknes seized, and whose endeavors to be virtuous were constantly obstructed by other beings containing souls formed from corrupt matter.

Upon this absurd and fanciful foundation Manichæus erected a superstructure, asserting that, in order to obviate the power of these latter beings, the Supreme Being produced two superior emanations, the Son and the Holy Ghost, consubstantial with the Father, but subordinate to Him, who exert their benign influence upon the bodies and souls of men; that God sent good angels and prophets upon earth to instruct man, and at length his own Son, who took upon Him the appearance, not the nature, of man, thereby denying the reality of the crucifixion and resurrection. But it were next to impossible to recount all the impious tenets of this heresiarch, insomuch that Pope Leo said of him that the devil reigned in all other heresies, but had raised his very throne in that of the Manichæans, who embraced all the errors and impieties that the spirit of man was capable of. They were divided into hearers and elect; of the elect, twelve were called Masters, in imitation of the twelve Apostles, and there was a kind of Pope amongst them. It would seem that Manichæism made great progress in Egypt; for Diocletian issued a sanguinary decree against the professors of it in the year 296, in reply to a letter from the proconsul of Africa.

DIOCLETIAN.

Diocletian assumed the imperial purple in the year 284. The tranquility which, after the Decian persecution, had with little interruption soothed and recruited the Church, continued through several years of Diocletian's reign. The Christians publicly professed their religous sentiments; they were openly received at court, and their opinions were professed by the favorite domestics of the monarch, through whom they were exonerated from making their appearance at the heathen sacrifices, a test which had before been imposed upon all persons in places of power and trust. Under these circumstances Christianity greatly increased; multitudes daily embraced it, and edifices for public worship sprang up on every side. But it soon had to pass through the ordeal of another most bloody persecution.

THE HIERACITES.

Towards the close of the third century, about the year 296, the sect of Hieracites was formed in Egypt by one Hierax, whose notions have sometimes being erroneously confounded with those of Manes. Believing that the great business of Christ was to promulgate a new law, more perfect and more strict than that of Moses, he prohibited the use of wine, flesh, marriage, and whatever was grateful to the senses. Yet possibly he supposed that severe injunctions of this nature were imposed by Christ only upon those who aspired to the highest attainments in virtue. He denied the resurrection; excluded children dying before years of discretion from the kingdom of Heaven; distinguished the substance of the Son from that of the Father; taught that Melchisedech was the Holy Ghost; obscured the Sacred Volume with allegorical interpretations; and maintained that Paradise was no sensible thing, but only the joy and satisfaction of the soul.

TENTH GENERAL PERSECUTION.

In the year 286, Diocletian associated with himself in the empire Maximianus Herculius, with the title Augustus. Diocletian, living at Necomedia, in Asia Minor, undertook the management of Egypt and the East; while Maximian, living at Milan, superintended Italy and Africa. At a later period, about 291, the two emperors strengthened themselves by choosing two coadjutors, Constantius Chlorus and Galerius, who exercised a somewhat inferior authority under the title of Cæsars. Constantius ruled in Spain, Gaul, and Britain, and Galerius in Illyria and the Danubian provinces. Under these four associated emperors the Church at first had peace; but at length the calm was interrupted, and a persecution more bloody than any which had gone before began, and lasted for ten years. A foretaste of what was coming was experienced in 298, when an edict was issued to the effect that all persons in office about the court or in the army should be present at the heathen sacrifices. Constantinus was the only one of the four heads of the empire who had no part in this order. But it was not until the year 303 that the Diocletian (more correctly the Galerian) persecution broke out in its fury. Galerius, instigated partly by his own inclination and partly by pagan priests (who declared that the oracles and omens were marred by the presence of Christians), obtained from his father-in-law, Diocletian, who was then at Nicomedia, an edict enjoining that the churches and books of the Christians should be destroyed, and all their rights and privileges as Roman citizens annulled. The attempt to exterminate the Scriptures was a new feature in this persecution. Many Christians refused to comply with the terms of the edict and suffered death. Those who, to save their lives, gave up their books, were stigmatized by their more resolute brethren, with the title of *traditores*. No sooner was the edict published than the church of Nicomedia was demolished, and the copies of the sacred books burned. Irritated at this, a Christian tore down the edict from the conspicuous position in which it was placed, and suffered for his temerity by being roasted alive. A dreadful fire in the palace of Nicomedia was attributed to the Christians, who were put to horrible torments in consequence. This catastrophe was succeeded by several edicts against the Christians, ordering that all Bishops should be thrown into prison, and by all ways imaginable compelled to sacrifice; and subsequently that all Christians should sacrifice to the gods, or be put to the torture. The most fiery of all the trials which the Church had undergone now approached, and persecution raged with unbounded fury throughout the empire, except in Gaul and Britain, where Constantius protected the persons of the Christians, although he allowed demolition of the Churches. Human imagination was almost exhausted in inventing a variety of tortures. Some were impaled alive; some were roasted by slow fires; some had melted lead poured down their throats; some had their flesh torn off with shells; and some had splinters of reeds thrust under their nails. Those who were not capitally punished had their features and limbs mutilated. It would be endless to enumerate the victims. The Bishops of Nicomedia, Tyre, Sidon, and Emesa; many matrons and virgins of the purest character; and a nameless multitude of plebeians arrived at immortality through the flames of martyrdom. Wearied at length with contention, or moved by the excruciating anguish which he himself suffered from a loathsome disease, Galerius, in the year 311, after the abdication of Diocletian, indulged his Christian subjects with a transient respite from their sufferings, and issued an edict permitting them to have buildings for religious worship. His successor, however, continued the persecution, though with some intermission and mitigation, until Constantine became invested with the sole dominion of the Roman world.

THE MELETIAN SCHISM.

The Meletians were so called from Meletius, Bishop of Lycopolis, in Egypt, who was deposed by the Council of Alexandria because he had sacrificed in the Diocletian persecution. After his deposition, however, Meletius continued to assume the title and exercise the functions of his office; and when Peter, Bishop of Alexandria, sought safety by flight, Meletius took upon himself to make certain regulations connected with Peter's office, and ordain persons to the ministry. The schism distracted the Church for many years. Meletius himself was prohibited forever by the Council of Nice, but his followers were admitted to communion without re-ordination.

II. THE FOURTH CENTURY.

THE DONATISTS.

The schism of the Donatists is the most important that disturbed the Church in the early part of the fourth century. Cæcilianus, the Archdeacon of Carthage, on the demise of Mensurius, Bishop of that See, in the year 311, was consecrated to the vacant office by some of the African bishops, without waiting for the assent of the bishops of Numidia. These prelates, offended at the slight, cited Cæcilianus to appear before them and defend himself, at Carthage; upon his refusing to submit to their authority, he was deposed, and his deacon, Marjorinus, ordained by them in his room, on the following grounds :— (1) That he refused to appear before the Council; (2) That Felix of Aptunga, the principal bishop who assisted at his consecration, was a *traditor*; (3) That during the Diocletian persecution he had behaved with inhumanity to the Christians who were in prison. Donatus was the leader of the party who opposed Cæcilianus; hence the name Donatists. A council of Bishops summoned by Constantine to meet at Rome under Melchiades Bishop of Rome, decided that Cæcilianus was the rightful Bishop of Carthage. Another council was held at Arles (at, which three British bishops were present), A. D. 314; also confirmed the election of Cæcilianus, who was consequently recognized by the Catholic Church as the legitimate bishop of Carthage. But the schismatics refused to acquiesce in the decision of the council, and continued to elect bishops of their own and the schism was not quite extinct until the seventh century.

CONVERSION OF CONSTANTINE.

Constantius, the father of Constantine, had shown himself favorably disposed to the Christian cause, and Constantine gave early indications of a desire to protect its professors, but at the same time he liberally enriched the temples of the gods and publicly worshipped at their shrines. The conversion of Constantine is said to have been miraculous, and is generally ascribed to the year 312, when he was master of Spain and Gaul, and went against Maxentius in Italy, who was reigning tyrannically in Rome. It is related on the testimony of Eusebius (*Life of Constantine*, B. 1, chap. 29–31), who says he had it from the emperor himself, that as the army of Constantine approached Rome, about three o'clock in the afternoon, there suddenly appeared a pillar of light in the heavens, in the fashion of a cross, with this inscription upon it — Τούτῳ νίκα, *by this conquer*. The emperor was confounded by this vision, and knew not what it meant; but our Saviour appeared to him in a dream to confirm the prognostic of the luminous phenomenon, commanding him to make a standard like that which he had seen in the heavens, and cause it to be carried before him in war as an ensign of victory and safety. Though the story itself has very generally obtained credit, yet the extraordinary appearances connected with it may well be questioned. One thing, however, is certain. About that period, and possibly on that occasion, a standard (called Labarum) was made. This was adorned with a crown, a cross, and a monogram of the name of Christ, and in subsequent years employed to excite the enthusiasm of the Christian soldiers. Constantine soon afterwards defeated Maxentius and entered Rome in triumph. He caused a statue of himself to be erected, with a cross in his right hand, and an inscription which attributed the liberation of the city to that saving emblem; and he ordered that for the future no man should suffer the death of the Cross, which till now was looked upon as the most ignominious of all others.

SUBSEQUENT ACTS OF CONSTANTINE.

Having settled affairs at Rome, Constantine joined his colleague Licinius at Milan, whence a joint edict was issued, authorizing every subject of the empire to profess his own religion unmolested, especially securing to the Christians their places of public worship, and directing the restoration of whatever property they had been dispossessed of by the late persecution. Hostility subsequently broke out between the two emperors, and a war ensued which ended in the death of Licinius. It does not appear that Constantine became a true Christian from the time of "the vision of the Cross:" at first he only tolerated Christianity, allowing it an equal footing with paganism. But, when he was left in undisputed possession of the dominions of Rome by the death of Licinius, he had arrived at a sounder faith, and exerted his authority to establish Christianity. He removed the seat of empire to Byzantium, which he embellished and enlarged, erecting there many glorious churches, honoring it with his own name, and prohibiting within it the performance of any pagan rites and ceremonies. His religious zeal augmented with his years; and without having received the initiatory rite of baptism he performed many of the solemn ceremonies appointed by the Church. In his last illness he summoned several bishops, fervently requesting to receive from them the sacrament of Baptism, which was administered to him by Eusebius, Bishop of Nicomedia. Constantine expired in the year 337, at the age of 64.

ARIANISM.

About the year 319, a storm arose in Egypt, which subsequently spread its ravages over the Christian world. Alexander, Bishop of Alexandria, in discoursing upon the subject of the Unity of the Divine Trinity, maintained among other things than the Son is not only of the same dignity, but of the same *essence* as the Father. Arius, a presbyter of Alexandria, and an unsuccessful candidate for the bishopric, influenced possibly by illwill towards Alexander on that account, considered that Alexander's position was allied to Sabellianism and going into the opposite extreme maintained that the Son is totally and *essentially* distinct from the Father.

He taught that the Son was begotten before all worlds, but that there had been a time when He was not; and therefore, that He is inferior to the

Father both in nature and dignity. He defended his heresy by showing that "if the Father begat the Son, He who was begotten had a beginning of existence, therefore once the Son did not exist, therefore He is formed from what once was not." And thus, by a sophism drawn from the title of *Son*, Arius concluded against the very doctrine which that term was expressly intended to convey—the identity of nature between the Second Person and the First.

The party of Arius soon became considerable; it was countenanced by two bishops, and by many distiguished for rank and abilities. Alexander, after exhorting the apostate presbyter to renounce his error, assembled a council of a hundred bishops, by whom his opinion was publicly condemned. The condemnation was ratified by a Synod of Egyptian and Libyan bishops; and the heresiarch with his adherents was excommunicated. Not discouraged, Arius retired into Palestine, where he made considerable accessions to his cause. The historian Eusebius and others attempted to mediate, but Alexander withstood all their intercessions.

THE COUNCIL OF NICE.

The Arian disputes attracted the attention of Constantine, who endeavored to compose them. But as the words of the emperor were not sufficiently powerful to extinguish the flame, in the year 325 he convened the celebrated Council of Nice in Bithynia, at which were debated (1) the Arian controversy; (2) the time of keeping Easter; and (3) the Meletian schism. At this council it is supposed that 318 bishops were present: it sat probably about two months, though some say two years. The doctrines of Arius were condemned, and the Son declared to be consubstantial, or of the same substance ($\delta\mu oo\acute{u}\sigma\iota o\varsigma$, homoousios), and not of like substance ($\delta\mu o\iota o\acute{u}\sigma\iota o\varsigma$, homœusios) with the Father; and Arius himself was banished to Illyria, but the emperor recalled him at the expiration of three years. The Homoousian faith, or doctrine of Consubstantiality, was at first opposed, or at least received with hesitation, by some bishops — the most eminent of them being Eusebius of Nicomedia (and afterwards of Constantinople), and his namesake Eusebius of Cæsarea. The council settled the Paschal controversy by deciding in favor of the custom of the Western Church; and it condemned the Meletian schism.

BISHOPS IN THE EARLY CHURCH.

ROME.

	A.D.
1. Linus	58
2. Anacletus	68
3. Clement	93
4. Evaristus	100
5. Alexander	109
6. Sixtus or Xystus	119
7. Telesphorus	128
8. Hyginus	138
9. Pius	142
10. Anicetus	156
11. Soter	168
12. Eleutherus	173
13. Victor	190
14. Zephyrinus	201
15. Calistus or Calixtus	218
16. Urbanus	222
17. Pontianus	230
18. Anterus } 19. Fabianus }	238
20. Cornelius	251
21. Lucius	252
22. Stephen	253
23. Sixtus II	257
24. Dionysius	259
25. Felix	269
26. Eutychianus	274
27. Caius	283
28. Marcellinus	296
29. Marcellus	308
30. Eusebius } 31. Melchiades }	310
32. Sylvester	314

JERUSALEM.

	A.D.
1. James	32
2. Symeon	62
3. Justus	104

ANTIOCH.

1. Evodius	43
2. Ignatius	70
3. Heros	107

ALEXANDRIA.

1. Mark	58
2. Annianus	62
3. Abilius	82
4. Cerdo	97
5. Primus	108
6. Justus	120
7. Eumenes	131
8. Marcus	143
9. Celadion	153
10. Agrippinus	168
11. Julianus	181
12. Demetrius	188
13. Heraclas	232
14. Dionysius	247
15. Maximus	265
16. Theanas	282
17. Peter	300
18. Achillas	312
19. Alexander	315

ATHENS.

1. Dyonisius.
2. Publius.
3. Quadratus.

HERETICS.

FIRST CENTURY.

Judaizing — Nazarenes, Ebionites and Nicolaitans.
Gnostic — Simonians, Cerinthians, Menandrians, and Docetæ.

SECOND CENTURY.

Asiatic Gnostics — Saturninus, Tatian, Bardesanes, and Elxai.
Alexandrian Gnostics — Basilides, and Valentinus.

There were also Cerdon, Marcion, Carpocrates, Theodotus, Praxeas, Artemon, Montanus.

THIRD CENTURY.

Novatus, Sabellius, Paul of Samosata, Manes, and Beryllus. There were also the schisms of Felicissimus and Novatus, and controversies on the Lapsed and on baptism by heretics.

APOLOGISTS.

The Apologists (all of whom flourished in the second century) were Quadratus (125), Aristides (125), Justin Martyr (148), Melito (166), Athenagoras (167), Miltiades, Apollinarius, Theophilus of Antioch, and Tatian.

PERSECUTIONS.

Historians generally reckon ten Persecutions of the Christians under Roman Emperors, namely,

		A. D.			A. D.
1. Under	Nero	64– 68	6. Under Maximinus		235
2. "	Domitian	94– 96	7. "	Decius	249–253
3. "	Trajan	104–117	8. "	Valerian	257–260
4. "	Hadrian	118	9. "	Aurelian	272
5. "	Severus	202–211	10. "	Diocletian	303–313

The term "Father" is applied to those early Christian writers who were regarded in their day as authorities in doctrine and practice, and in whose writings we find the history, doctrines and traditions of the early Church. These are as follows:

APOSTOLIC FATHERS.

	A. D.		A. D.
Barnabas, died about	57	Ignatius, died about	117
Clemens, " "	100	Hernas, " "	150

Polycarp, died about..........A. D. 167.

CHURCH FATHERS.

	A. D.		A. D.
Dionysius, died about	100	Tertullian, died about	220
Hermias, " "	150	Minutius Felix, " "	225
Justin Martyr " "	167	Origen, " "	254
Tatian, " "	176	Cyprian, " "	258
Hegesippus, " "	180	Dionysius of Alexandria	265
Theophilus, " "	182	Gregory Thaumaturgus	270
Athenagoras, " "	190	Victorinus, died about	303
Irenæus, " "	202	Arnobius, " "	326
Hippolytus, " "	210	Lactantius, " "	330
Clemens of Alexandria	220		

CHAPTER IV.

From the Council at Nice till the Birth of Martin Luther.
A. D. 324–1483.

1. THE FOURTH CENTURY.—Continued.

DEATH OF CONSTANTINE.

Constantine died in 337, and was buried in the Church of the Apostles at Constantinople. Constantine II. and Constans became emperors of the West, and Constantius emperor in the East. The Union between the Church and the State now became more intimate. The emperors convened and presided over the councils of the Church; confirmed their decrees; enacted ecclesiastical laws themselves; decided concerning heresies and controversies; appointed bishops, and inflicted punishment for violation of church-laws.

JULIAN.

In 361 Julian, the Apostate, was crowned. He renounced the Christian faith, and endeavored to establish paganism; he wrote against Christianity and forbade Christians to teach the liberal arts and sciences. He was killed in battle in 363, and Christianity was immediately re-established.

ARIANISM.—THE ROMAN SEE.

During the reign of Theodosius I., the Great, A. D. 379–395, there was a decline and fall of Arianism. The tenets were, however, maintained among barbarians—Vandals, Goths, Lombards—until the middle of the seventh century. Choral singing introduced at this time by Ambrose, and the Latin translation of the Scriptures improved. Extension of the power of the Roman See. Doctrine of purgatory taught at beginning of fifth century. Augustine thinking Origen's view of the purification of souls by fire between death and the judgment in all probability correct. Extensive conversion of the Gauls; great spread of the Gospel in Germany.

PELAGIANISM.—ABUSES.

Controversy between Pelagius and Augustine. Pelagius denied the doctrine of original sin, the total corruption of human nature, irresistible grace, and absolute decrees of election. Opposed by Augustine, who contended for all these. Pelagius taught his views at Rome. His system condemned by the Synods of Mylene and Carthage. Semi-Pelagianism in Gaul. Period of violent controversy, pompous ceremonial, rising secular power, and growing corruption of the Church. General religious decline. Increasing wealth in the Church. Only a few heathen-temples remained; the heathen excluded from posts of honor.

NOTE.—The author of Pelagianism was a native of Wales, named Morgan, which signifies *sea-born;* whence his Latin name Pelagius. In early life he went to Rome, and there imbibed errors which he afterwards propagated in Africa and the East. His principal errors were a denial of the original corruption of human nature, and of the necessity of Divine grace —holding that man can of his own will turn unto God, and work out his salvation. The opinions of Pelagius were condemned by councils at Carthage, A. D. 412; at Ephesus A. D. 431; and subsequently by the council of Orange, A. D. 529. Agricola, the son of a Bishop of Gaul, is said to have brought his doctrines into Britain, Pelagius himself never having revisited his native country. The native bishops, unable to cope with their antagonists, besought the aid of the Gallic Church to arrest the spread of Pelagianism; whereupon Germanus, Bishop of Auxerre, and Lupus, Bishop of Troyes, came over. They held a conference with the Pelagians at St. Albans, in which the latter were put to silence.

A favorable condition of this century was the fact that far from Rome the Gospel was making its way among the simple tribes of barbarians, and here were shortly to be its greatest triumphs. It has been truly said that when the northern barbarians came down upon old Rome and took away forever her world-wide authority, nothing then saved the world from a lapse into utter barbarism except the Christian Church, which, coming to the rescue, so wrought by the subtle agency of spiritual forces that the conquerors were themselves conquered and became Christians. It may be as truly said that the same invasion was an immense blessing to the Church, in that it not only brought into her an element of strength with the accession of the converted Germanic tribes, but it also put before the Church something to do—and an immense task, too,—in Christianizing them, and thus turned her thoughts from sinful luxury, pride and strife.

The spread of the Gospel was less extensive in this age than the previous one. But the Armenian church was now formed; and the province of Armenia converted to Christ. An entrance was also made in Abyssinia, and the germs of the Gospel planted there. Iberia, now Georgia, in southeastern Europe, was Christianized through the efforts of a female slave who was carried to that province, and is said to have performed wonderful miracles. This, too, was the time of Ulphilas, Martin of Tours, and other equally noble men who through faith wrought righteousness, subdued kingdoms, and left a record which goes far to redeem the century from dishonor

II. THE FIFTH CENTURY.

In the fifth century the Nestorians of the mountain districts in Persia and northward, received the Gospel and became a Christian people. They were much persecuted by the Persians, but afterward more tolerance was granted them, by the interference, in their behalf, of Roman emperors.

The Armenians also received the Scriptures translated into their own language, about the beginning of the fifth century, the alphabet being invented for the purpose.

Among the German nations the Gospel made rapid progress; the Suevi and Alans in Spain and Portugal, the Visigoths of southern Gaul, the Burgundians, the Vandals of north Africa, and fragments of lesser peoples mingled with them, became Christians at increasingly rapid rate, and nearly all adopted the Arian doctrine.

Ireland was largely Christianized in this century by Patrick and his fellow preachers.

In Britain the Gospel spread among the people; schools were established, and the beginnings of an ecclesiastical system were made. A cathedral was built at Llandoff and a monastery founded at Bangor. The Isle of Man was made the scene of the labors of Germanus. But the primitive British Church was broken up and driven into Wales, Northumberland, etc., by the Anglo-Saxon invasion and conquest about the middle of the century

The Gospel was preached in Tyrol by Valentinus, in Austria and Bavaria by Severinus.

Toward the close of the century the persecution in Africa became very severe, and two hundred bishops were driven from Africa. As an offset to this, the Franks embraced Christianity after the battle of Tolbiac, and Clovis, the king, was baptized with 3,000 of his subjects.

III. THE SIXTH CENTURY.

THE ENGLISH CHURCH.

The English, as distinguished from the British, Church was founded by Augustine (commonly called Austin) at the close of the sixth century. Augustine was a Roman monk, who, together with forty others, was sent over to Britain, to convert the heathen Saxons, by Pope Gregory, in the year 596. The success of these missionaries, who landed in the Isle of Thanet, was very satisfactory. They converted Ethelbert, king of Kent; whose example was soon followed by the kings of Essex and Northumbria, and gradually by the other sovereigns of the Saxon heptarchy. Not long after his arrival in Britain, Augustine repaired to Arles, in France, where he was consecrated Archbishop of Canterbury, with the title of Legate of the Pope. It is supposed that at this time there were seven bishops of the British Church still existing, subject to the Archbishopric of Caerleon, or St. David's. Augustine, in a council held at Worcester, proposed union with them on the following conditions: — (1) that they should accord with the Western Church in the time of keeping Easter; (2) that they should adopt the Roman ritual in the administration of baptism; and (3) that they should submit to the authority of the Bishop of Rome. These terms were rejected, and the British bishops refused to acknowledge Augustine for their Archbishop, who had already assumed superiority by not deigning to rise from his seat to receive them, when they entered the council chamber. It was not until the year 755 that the ancient British Church conformed in these points to the Anglo-Saxon and Roman Churches. The whole country having been converted, dissensions sprang up in the Church, in consequence of which certain Anglo-Saxon kings sent a priest named Wighard to Rome, to be there canonically consecrated Archbishop of Canterbury. Wighard, however, died at Rome, and the pope, on the strength of the letters that Wighard had brought with him, consecrated in his stead a learned monk of Tarsus, named Theodore, whom he despatched to England in the year 669. The Saxon kings confirmed his appointment, and granted to the See of Canterbury the primacy over the English Church. Theodore healed the dissensions that existed, corrected abuses, and established discipline. He introduced the practice of holding councils, and encouraged the building of churches apart from monasteries by allowing the founders to become patrons of them.

In this century we have the downfall of the Western Roman Empire; central and eastern Europe overspread by the Sclavic race; great vices among the clergy; the bishop of Rome first received the title of "Pope"; clerical celibacy demanded by the edicts of Justinian; and the Scots Christianized by Columba of Ireland.

IV. THE SEVENTH CENTURY.

MOHAMMEDANISM.

Mohammed was born at Mecca, Arabia, in 569 or 570. 1. He declared himself a prophet, 609; 2. Fled to Medina, 622; 3. Founded a new religion, based on the Koran (collected by Abu Bekr in 635), which he wrote; 4. Conquered all Arabia; died from poison, 632. He was succeeded by Caliphs, who carried their victories over vast regions, until Egypt, Syria, Persia, North Africa, Asia Minor, Northern India, all Spain, and the south of France were under their dominion. Charles Martel arrested the progress of the Mohammedans in western Europe by a victory at Tours, France, A. D. 732. According to the monkish legends, three hundred thousand Moslems were killed. While the number slain was greatly exaggerated, the victory was yet complete and perpetual. Mohammedanism still prevails in the northern half of Africa, Turkey in Europe, Arabia, Persia, the Holy Land, and Asia Minor.

Brief Survey of Mohammedanism. Six chief doctrines: 1. The one God. 2. Angels and archangels. 3. The Koran. 4. The positive prophetical character of Mohammed and his successors. 5. Resurrection and the general judgment. 6. God's absolute predetermination of good and evil. The four great duties are: 1) Prayer. 2) Almsgiving. 3) Fasting. 4) Pilgrimages to Mecca and Medina. 5) Polygamy. 6) Prohibition to eat swine-meat.

GREGORY THE GREAT.

Gregory the Great was Bishop of Rome, A. D. 590–604. He called himself the "Servant of the servants of our Lord." He magnified the pretensions of the Roman See; revised the ritual; promoted monastic life and institutions; patronized church music and ceremonial observances; cultivated theological literature, strict clerical discipline, and almsgiving; discouraged the liberal sciences; and established purgatory as a positive doctrine. Gregory sent monks into Britain for the re-conversion of the Anglo-Saxons. He was incited to do so by the beauty of some English boys, whom he had seen in the Roman slave market. The mission conducted by the monk Augustine, first Archbishop of Canterbury.

V. THE EIGTH CENTURY.

THE VENERABLE BEDE.

The most learned and celebrated writer of the early English Church was the Venerable Bede, who lived and died an humble recluse in the monastery of Jarrow, in Northumberland, where he was born in the year 671. His life was devoted to the attainments of varied knowledge, diversified only by the monastic exercises of psalmody, prayer, and manual labor. His works, which consist of commentaries on Scripture, homilies, lives of Saints, an admirable history of the Church of England from the mission of Augustine to his own time, and other treatises, fill eight folio volumes. Bede died in the year 734, at the age of sixty-three.

In the beginning of this century masses were said for the dead, the sick, and for fine weather. Pilgrimages to Rome became of much importance. And the ecclesiastical authority predominated over the secular power.

REIGN OF CHARLEMAGNE.

Charlemagne, first as participant in the general government, and finally as the emperor of the West. He reigned A. D. 768-814. He propagated Christianity among the Franks by force. Alcuin, his friend and adviser, commended milder measures, but to no purpose. He was sole emperor of the Franks A. D. 771. Carried on wars against the Saxons, Bohemians, and Huns. Gave increased grants of land to the papacy; was, nevertheless, acknowledged by the pope as supreme. Great patron of learning; founded the University of Paris; had the best books of theology, philosophy, and literature read to him; was himself a very diligent student, with Alcuin as teacher. He organized a revision and correction of the Latin version of the Scriptures.

CONTROVERSIES.

Rise of the Adoption Controversy in Spain, that Christ is not the true Son of God, but, according to his human nature, Son of God only by adoption. This view was an accommodation to the prejudices of the Mohammedan inhabitants of Spain. Forgery of the false Isidorean decretals, granting important concessions to the papacy. The Aristotelian philosophy in high favor in the East. The establishment of transubstantiation—that the bread and wine at the Lord's Supper became really the body and blood of Christ.

VI. NINTH, TENTH, AND ELEVENTH CENTURIES.

NINTH CENTURY.

Early in the ninth century the Nestorian patriarch of Syria sent missionaries to China and the East Indies.

In 812 the Normans invaded Britain and slew hundreds and probably several thousands of monks, and broke up many churches, and destroyed towns. They also ravaged certain districts on the Baltic coast.

Missions were pushed in Jutland and throughout Scandinavia,

Bohemia, Bulgaria, and among the Tartars in the Crimea. In Scandinavia the remaining leaders of the Norse heathen tried in vain to stay the progress of Christianity. In Bulgaria Mohammedanism became a rival of Christianity and gained some adherents. In Moravia, Cyril and Methodius, with some difficulty and opposition, prepared a translation of the Scripture and the liturgy, but the Slavonic liturgy was gradually supplanted, all through Bohemia, Hungary and Poland, by the Latin rite. Progress was slow in all these districts.

TENTH CENTURY.

The beginning of the tenth century saw a better state of things, politically, in Europe. While learning had declined so much as to be almost entirely neglected, and the hierarchy had become hopelessly entangled and degraded, there arose at that time, a new German empire, when Otho the Great took the reins in 936, which lasted until Henry IV., 1056, during which time Germany became conscious of existence, and of a centre of unity; the Normans were held in check, the Hungarians reduced to quiet and order, and the northern nations of Europe were Christianized — the previous work being then brought together, completed, and its results systematized.

Missions in the East may be said to have ended with the ninth century. The breach between Rome and Constantinople was constantly widening and the eastern Church was sinking into an oriental supineness and superstition.

The persecutions by the remnants of Norse heathenism were quelled. Bohemia made a fierce fight, but was subdued by Otho after fourteen years of resistance.

Russia was entered and some vigorous work done by the Greek Church, resulting eventually in the establishment of Greek Christianity throughout the empire, Vladimir the Great, 980, abolished the last vestiges of paganism.

Finally about 997, several missionaries journeyed to the Faroe and Shetland Islands, and to Iceland, and Christianized the Islands, founded a bishopric, and organized a mission from Iceland to Greenland, which began operations in 999.

ELEVENTH CENTURY.

In the eleventh century Denmark, Sweden, Norway, Russia, and Poland, all became confirmed in the Christian faith and measures were taken to destroy all remnants of heathenism. In Hungary, Transylvania and Wallachia, missions were vigorously pushed. Pomerania, in 1066, killed the Christian founder of the kingdom, and exterminated every trace of Christianity. And in Prussia, Bruno and eighteen companions were put to death for their zeal in missions.

Generally, there was little done in the eleventh century, in extending the kingdom of Christ. In the east the Turks and Saracens became exceedingly oppressive; in the west Christianity was established everywhere except in the south of Spain, in Prussia, the north of Sweden, and parts of Russia.

HILDEBRAND, OR GREGORY VII.

The celebrated Hildebrand, a man of humble origin, but undaunted spirit and confident zeal, ascended the papal throne in the year 1073, and assumed the title of Gregory VII. He was the first to develop fully the idea of the papal supremacy, by carrying out the principles of the *False Decretals.*

NOTE.—The *False Decretals*, a collection of letters on ecclesiastical laws, which purported to have been written by the Bishops of Rome from the time of Clement down to the year 614, and in which the judgments of all bishops, the holding of all councils, and a right to hear appeals from all ecclesiastical judgments were claimed for the Roman pontiffs. These decretal epistles, which are now acknowledged by the most learned Romanists to be mere fabrications, exaggerated to the highest degree the powers and privileges of the popes. The ignorance which prevailed in these early times prevented any discovery of their falsehood, and they gradually became the groundwork of the papal canon-law.

VI. THE TWELFTH AND THIRTEENTH CENTURIES.

TWELFTH CENTURY.

The twelfth century was the age of crusades. Almost nothing else was done in the way of missions. Boleslas, of Poland, conquered Pomerania, and established Christianity there. The Slavonic Wends were also subdued by Albert of north Saxony;

and the northern Wends by the so-called Saxon crusade under Henry the Lion.

The first Crusade was undertaken in 1096, when Pope Urban II. persuaded the councils of Placentia and Clermont to order the undertaking. About 300,000 men joined themselves to the regular army of 400,000, which was chiefly French, and started after Peter the Hermit and Walter the Penniless. Most of the 300,000 perished in Bohemia. The regular army under Gofrey of Bouillon, Hugh, Robert of Normandy, and Robert of Flanders, pushed on, and at length captured Jerusalem.

The second Crusade, in 1144, was incited by St. Bernhard. Louis VII. of France, and Conrad of Germany, led 1,200,000 men to ultimate ruin and death.

The third was the largest of all. Saladin captured Jerusalem in 1187. Gregory VIII. called all Catholic Europe to recapture the city. The Emperor Frederick, Philip of France, and Richard cour de Leon led the army, which finally took Jerusalem, but was itself destroyed.

Fourth Crusade, A. D. 1203.—Determined upon by Pope Innocent III. Christendom not in a condition to organize one. The beginnings of an army met at Venice, but never went to Palestine. Baldwin, Count of Flanders, leader. Some writers claim as the fourth Crusade an expedition organized in 1217 by Andrew II., of Hungary, who, supported by the kings of Jerusalem and Cyprus, took a fortress and some forts on Mount Tabor, and returned home in 1218.

The Boy Crusade, A. D. 1212. — Conducted by Stephen of Vendôme, a shepherd boy. He was followed by 30,000 children of about twelve years of age. They set sail from Marseilles for Palestine in seven ships; two wrecked; the remainder reached Egypt, where the children were sold as slaves.

Fifth Crusade, A. D. 1228, 1229. — Commenced by Frederick II., emperor of Germany. Terminated in ten years by a treaty between him and the Sultan of Egypt, when Palestine was ceded to the emperor, who returned to Germany.

Sixth Crusade, A. D. 1248.—Palestine invaded by Turks in 1244; Jerusalem captured and pillaged. Crusade conducted by Louis IX., of France. Taken prisoner by Sultan of Egypt, but ransomed, and restored to liberty in 1250.

Seventh Crusade, A. D. 1270-1272.—First undertaken by St. Louis, of France, but after his death, in Tunis, conducted by Edward I., of England. Failure; return of Edward to England. The country in possession of the Mohammedans.

THE PAPAL POWER IN ENGLAND.

The Church of England smarted severely under the papal tyranny; dut there are few instances of it in England before the Norman conquest. The pope, however, made a pretext of his support of William I. in his invasion of that country for enlarging his encroachments, and in that king's reign began to send legates there. William, however, refused to take the oath of fidelity to the Pope and his successors, as he required by the papal legate. In baronial times, bishops were regarded as tennants in chief of the crown, and the investiture of them by delivery of the staff and ring (symbolic of their pastoral office and union with their churches), continued to be strenuously insisted on by the crown, until the popes began to be scandalized by the apparent transmission of a spiritual function through a lay channel. This was the cause of frequent contention, till at last the pope prevailed with Henry I. (1100-1135) to part with the right of nominating to bishoprics, the king only reserving to himself the ceremony of homage. And it was agreed that, for the future, none should be invested by the king or lay patron, in any preferment, by the pastoral staff and ring; that no one, elected to a prelacy, should be denied consecration on account of his rendering homage to the Crown. In the reign of Stephen (1135-1154) he gained the prerogative of appeals; and as the jurisdiction of the Church extended in those ages to a great number of temporal causes, vast sums of money were in this way continually draining out of England. He exempted all clerks from the secular power in the reign of Henry II. (1154-1189), who at first strenuously opposed the innovation; but after the murder of Thomas à Becket, Archbishop of Canterbury, the pope (who had all along made Becket's quarrel with the king that of the Holy See) succeeded, and

Henry appeased the wrath of the Church of Rome by performing a severe penance (for a crime in which he had no share) at Becket's tomb. Not long after this, in the reign of John (1199-1216), upon the occasion of the pope's appointment of Stephen Langton to the archbishopric of Canterbury, another struggle occurred respecting the investiture of the bishops. Upon this occasion the pope (Innocent III.) laid the kingdom under an interdict, and finding this to fail in producing the intended effect, he proceeded to pass the sentence of excommunication against the king; and, in the following year, declared the king of England deposed from his dignity, and the people absolved from their allegiance. John was reduced to such straits that he surrendered his kingdom and crown to the pope, consenting to hold them of him under a rent of a thousand marks, and gave up in effect the disposal of all bishoprics in England to the pope. By such exaction as these Innocent managed either to *provide* or appoint beforehand to benefices as vacancies might occur; or to *reserve* to himself the right of promoting to vacant benefices. By means of this iniquitous system of *provisions* and *reservations* absentee foreigners held most of the richest benefices in the reign of Henry III. (1216-1272): and partly from this cause, and partly from the taxes imposed by the pope, there went yearly out of that kingdom seventy thousand pounds sterling — an immense sum in those days. During this period the discipline of the Church and morals of the laity were corrupted by the sale of plenary indulgencies and pardons.

DECLENSION OF PAPAL SUPREMACY.

The first checks were given to the power of the Church of Rome in England in the early part of the reign of Edward I. In 1275 a statute was passed at Westminster, which provided that all clerks charged with felony should be tried by the civil power before they were delivered over to their ordinary or diocesan; and four years after this, in 1279, in consequence of the impoverishment of the king's exchequer by the accumulation of landed property (one-fifth, it is said, of the entire kingdom) in the hands of ecclesiastical bodies, whereby it became exempt from certain taxes, the statute of *Mortmain* made the king's consent necessary for the ratification of the transfer of such property to the Church. The number of English benefices held by foreigners induced Edward III., in 1351, to pass the statute of *Provisors*, by which it was enacted that the Bishop of Rome should not present to any benefice in England, but the patrons; and that fine and imprisonment should be imposed upon those who disturbed a patron in the presentation of a living by virtue of a papal provision. In the following year, 1352, parties suing in or appealing to the courts of the pope, and in 1392 parties procuring at Rome or elsewhere translations of prelates, processes, excommunications, bulls, or instruments which affect the king, his crown and realm, were made liable to the penalties of the statutes of *Præmunire* (the first of which was passed in the reign of Henry I.), namely, loss of the king's protection, forfeiture of goods, lands, and imprisonment during the king's will.

PAPAL CLAIMS TO AUTHORITY.

Dr. Corrie, in the supplemental matter to his edition of *Burnet's History of the Reformation*, recites the following as the principle claims to authority which the pope asserted with respect to England:—

1) A legislative power in ecclesiastical or spiritual causes.

2) A dispensing power above and against the laws of Church or State.

3) The exemption of criminous clerks from civil jurisdiction.

4) A right to send legates and hold legatine courts.

5) The right to receive appeals from the English courts.

6) The patronage of the English Church; and the investiture of the bishops of England, with power to require oaths from them contrary to the oath of allegiance to the sovereign.

7) The rights to the first fruits and tenths of ecclesiastical benefices.

8) The right to depose the sovereign of England, and release subjects from their oath of allegiance.

MONKS AND FRIARS.

The monks and begging friars were the most vehement supporters of the papal authority. The pope relieved them from the inspection of their bishops, and made them immediately subject to the papal see, which was in effect leaving them almost without control. For this reason they were advocates for the papal power in every diocese. Monastic life, originated in the Decian persecution; but it was not until the succeeding century that societies of monks, or monasteries, were formed. Originally, all monks were laymen: but in course of time one or more inmates of a monastery were ordained for the performance of divine service in the institution, and others were chosen by the bishops for the service of the Church. They were distinguished by the name of *regulares*, as living according to rules, *regulæ*; and such of them as were ordained to the priesthood were called *clerici regulares*, in contradistinction to the *clerici seculares*, or parish priests, so called as living according to the manners of the time, *seculum*. Friars (from *fratres*, brothers,) were monks not ordained to the priesthood. In the twelfth century, when the popular mind was growing a little jealous of the increase and wealth of the monasteries, which had acquired much property and innumerable benefices, small bodies of religious persons began to arrive in England. These were the mendicant friars, consisting of the four orders of Dominicans, Franciscans, Augustinians, and Carmelites, who exhibited for a time an ardent zeal, and a spirit of poverty and self-denial. They soon, however, intrenched upon the duties of the priesthood, and created much commotion in the country. They preached out of doors, railed at the resident pastor, and gave absolution to the black sheep of his flock, attacked the cathedral clergy, and so poisoned the minds of the people that Pentecostals began to be evaded, and it became a hard matter to keep the walls of God's temple in decent repair. They cast their stone, too, at the monks, contrasting their own affected poverty with the gallant bearing and ample retinues of the former. It were useless to endeavor here to give an account of all the villanies practised by the friars, until at length they became as rottenness to the bones of the Roman Church. The pope, however, continued his favor to them throughout, for they were the men of his right hand, and maintained his cause against every antagonist.

THE WALDENSES AND ALBIGENSES.

In the twelfth century there appeared a race of hardy mountaineers in the secluded valleys of the Alps, who held the essential articles of the reformed faith. They were called Voudois, Vallenses, or Waldenses. Their form of church government was episcopal; and the commandments (not excepting that against idols) and the worship of the Trinity (but not of the Virgin) were taught amongst them. They gave no credit to modern miracles; rejected extreme unction; held offerings for the dead as nothing worth; and denied the doctrines of transubstantiation, purgatory, and invocation of saints. It is not difficult to account for the transmission of the doctrine of the Waldenses to England. A section of them emigrated to Bohemia, between which country and England there was considerable intercourse about the time of Wickliffe: Bohemians were students at Oxford, and Richard II. chose a Bohemian princess for his Queen; some of whose retinue, returning to their native country after the Queen's decease, carried with them the writings of Wickliffe, and thus gave the first impulse to the movement in which Huss and Jerome became so conspicuous. Moreover, some of the persecuted race repaired to Provence and Languedoc, where they were known by the name of Albigenses, or heretics of Albi, at one time their principal seat. They were driven by the Inquisition and the sword into the neighboring English territory of Guienne, whence probably they found a way for themselves or their tenets into Britain.

THE INQUISITION.

This was a tribunal in the Roman Catholic Church for the discovery, repression, and punishment of heresy, unbelief, and other offences against religion. The first inquisitorial measure was adopted at the fourth Lateran Council in 1215, against a revival of the Albigenses. But the Synod of Toulouse, in 1229, was the first body to organize a regular Inquisition. All so-called heretics were hunted out with cruel persistence, and any Roman who spared one, was deprived of both office and property. Carod, of Marburg, the first grand Inquisitor of Germany was slain by a German noble.

VIII. THE FOURTEENTH CENTURY

JOHN WICKLIFFE.

The most terrible opponent the papacy had yet encountered in England was John Wickliffe, the Father of the English Reformers, who was born at Spreswell, near Richmond, Yorkshire, A. D. 1324. He probably received the rudiments of his education at one of the monasteries near Richmond, and at the age of sixteen was admitted a commoner of Queen's College, Oxford, but soon afterwards removed to Merton, where he obtained a fellowship. At Oxford, where he was "second to none in philosophy, and in scholastic discipline incomparable," he earned the title of the Evangelic or Gospel Doctor. In 1356 he published his first work, *The Last Age of the Church*, in which he inveighed against the covetousness of the papal court, and the profligacy of the clergy. Roused by the offensive pretentions of the mendicant friars, who had usurped the rights of the secular clergy, and advanced their conquests for the pope to an intolerable degree, he attacked them with great vigor in a tract in the year 1360. In 1365, Islip, the Primate, decided against the monks, and made him Warden of Canterbury Hall; but in the following year Archbishop Langham, who had succeeded Islip, and who favored the monks, expelled him, on account of his enmity to the friars. Wickliffe appealed to Rome. But at that time the Pope, Urban V., was attempting to revive the homage and tribute to which John had subjected this kingdom. Edward III. resisted the Pope's pretentions, his parliament supporting him, and declaring John's donation null and void, as being without the consent of Parliament and contrary to the coronation oath. Wickliffe stoutly maintained the king's cause; for which reason probably his appeal against the expulsion by Langham failed. Having taken his doctor's degree in 1372, he lectured on theology at Oxford, and attacked the abuses and errors of Romanism. While thus employed, he wrote a plain and popular "Exposition of the Decalogue,". and a series of short treatises called "The

Caitiff," and in 1374 he was sent as one of the king's commissioners to Bruges, to discuss with the popes nuncios certain grievances of the Church, the result of the discussion being an arrangment that the pope should desist from making use of reservations of benefices by his writ. Upon his return home, after an absence of two years upon this business, he was presented by the crown with the rectory of Lutterworth, in Leicestershire, and a prebendal stall in the collegiate Church of Westbury, Worcestershire. During his stay abroad he was made more sensible of the corruptions of the Romish Church, which he therefore the more boldly denounced, His endeavors to reform a corrupt age, and his dissemination of Scriptural doctrines, both by his own energetic preaching and by that of his "poor priests,' who went about collecting audiences in populous places, not only obtained him hosts of followers, but raised up against him many enemies. Nineteen articles (selected by the monks from his lectures and discourses), in which he was charged with broaching doctrines that were heretical and subversive of the Christian faith, were consequently exhibited against him to the Pope, Gregory XI., who issued bulls to Simon Sudbury, Archbishop of Canterbury, and William Courtney, Bishop of London, and also the University of Oxford, directing proceedings against him, A. D. 1377. The university suffered the bull to be neglected; and Sudbury likewise let several months elapse before he took any steps in the matter. But at length a mandate was issued by him in the joint names of himself and Courtney, addressed to the University of Oxford, requiring them to cite Wickliffe to appear before the prelates of St. Paul's. He appeared before this ecclesiastical court, and subsequently before another at Lambeth; but in neither case was any decision come to, owing perhaps to the conduct of Wickliffe's friends, John of Gaunt (Duke of Lancaster), and Henry Lord Percy (the Earl Marshall). The death of Gregory put an end to the commission, and that of Edward III. also tended to divert the thoughts of Wickliffe's enemies to other topics. On the accession of Richard II., the demand for the papal tribute was renewed, and Wickliffe once more roused the ire of the adherents of Rome by his oppositions to the claim. Having translated from the Vulgate (for he was unacquainted with the Hebrew and Greek originals) the Bible into English, he continued by lectures, sermons, and writings, to oppose the papal court and the vices of the clergy, in which he was doubtless encouraged both by the government and the people, and kept thereby comparatively free from persecution. But at length he openly attacked the great doctrine of transubstantiation, affirming that "the consecrated host which we see upon the altar is neither Christ nor any part of Him, but an effectual sign of Him, retaining after consecration the nature of bread," and that transubstantiation rested upon no Scriptural foundation. Upon this his supporters deserted him. The University of Oxford prohibited his teaching, upon pain of imprisonment, and the king in Parliament rejected his appeal against the decision of the University. Courtney had now succeeded Sudbury, who was killed in Wat Tyler's insurrection, in the primacy, and he convened a synod at the house of the Black Friars, in London A. D. 1382, which condemned Wickliffe's doctrines as heretical. For some time he withstood the tide of opposition and fury which now burst upon him; but he was eventually forced to quit the University and retire to his living at Lutterworth. Here he continued to promote the reformation of corruptions and to labor zealously as a parish priest until he received the final summons of his Heavenly Master in the year 1374, in the sixty-first year of his age, at a time when his enemies were designing to have him conveyed to Rome. The Roman see was bitterly opposed to the views of Wickliffe; and the Lateran council of Constance (1414–1418) condemned him with this sentence:—"That John Wickcliffe, being a notorious heretic, and obstinate, and dying in his heresy, his body and bones, if they may be discerned from the bodies of other faithful people, shall be taken out of the ground, and thrown away from the burial of the Church. The bishop of Lincoln, in early life a zealous adherent to the reformer, executed this sentence in 1425, causing Wickliffe's bones to be exhumed and burnt, and the ashes cast into a neighboring brook called the Swift. "The brook," says Fuller, "did convey his ashes into Avon, Avon into Severn; Severn into narrow seas; they into the main ocean. And thus the ashes of Wickliffe are the emblem of his doctrine, which now is dispersed all the world over."

JOHN HUSS.

Wickliffe's principles, had already spread in Bohemia, when his opposition to papal Rome began, by means of a Waldensian colony, and they were strengthened and extended by Oxford students who came over with the Bohemian Queen of Richard II. upon their return home. The information thus received from England sank deep into the heart of John Huss, who maintained them with wonderful zeal in the University of Prague, in which he was Professor of Theology, and Confessor to the Queen of Bohemia, and soon laid the foundation of a party extending through every gradation of society. This new and vigorous attack upon their tenets became a principal object of attention with the Divine assembled at the council of Constance, before whom Huss appeared. He was condemned as a heretic, and burnt alive in 1418, contrary to a safe-conduct granted to him by the Emperor Sigismund, which the council said it was not necessary to keep with a heretic. His friend and associate, Jerome of Prague, shared the same fate.

BURNING OF HERETICS.

It was a common thing in other parts of Europe to punish heresy with death, for nearly two centuries before a similar persecuting spirit showed itself in England. But Henry IV. ascended the throne with a defective title, and found it convenient to strengthen his position by conciliating the clergy. Accordingly, he encouraged the persecution of the Lollards, or Wickliffites, whose numbers had greatly increased; and in the year 1400 passed the statute *de hæretico cumburendo*, forbidding anyone to teach anything contrary to the Sacraments or the authority of the Church, under the penalty of being burnt before the people, the diocesan being appointed sole judge. The first victim of the law for burning heretics, and the martyr in the cause of the Reformation, was William Sautre, or Sawtrey, rector of St. Osyth's, London, formerly of Lynn, Norfolk. He was cited before Archbishop Arundel, and having refused to worship the cross of Christ, and denied the doctrine of transubstantiation, he was condemned as a heretic, and delivered over to the civil power for execution. The fatal notoriety of Smithfield commenced with the burning of Sautre, on the 26th of February, 1401. Thomas Badby, a tailor, of Worcester, was the second victim. He was burnt in Smithfield for refusing to abjure the Lollard opinion of the Eucharist, and denying the authority of the priesthood. The statute survived the Reformation nearly 150 years, and was not repealed till the year 1677, in the reign of Charles II.

REGINALD PECOCK.

A hateful system of private information was the consequence; but they were not wanting instances of persons in high places who were opposed to the persecuting spirit that prevailed. Of these perhaps Reginald Pecock (formerly of Oriel College, Oxford) is the most remarkable. He was born in 1390, and through the influence of his friend, Humphry, Duke of Gloucester, obtained the bishopric of St. Asaph in 1444, from which he was translated to Chichester in 1450. Acting upon his expressed opinion, that "the clergy would be condemned at the last day, if they did not draw men into consent to the true faith, otherwise than by fire and sword or hanging," he exerted himself in various ways, by tracts, and sermons, especially by a book called *The Repressor of over-much writing* (*i. e.*, blaming the Clergy), to win the Lollards, the great assailants of the Clergy), to many of whose tenets he was decidedly opposed, by argument rather than by persecution. In a work entitled *A Treatise of Faith*, he admitted that neither pope nor council can add to or change an article of the creed, inasmuch as Holy Scripture is the only ground of faith. This called down upon him the vengeance of the ruling party in the Church. He was expelled from the House of Lords in the year 1457, and cited to appear before the primate (Bourchier) at Lambeth Palace, where he was accused of maintaining that a belief in our Lord's descent into Hell, in the Holy Spirit, in the Catholic Church, in infallibility of the universal Church, in the authority of councils, &c., is not required of Christians. He was deposed from his bishopric, and compelled to recant at St. Paul's Cross, A. D. 1457. Having afterwards applied to the Pope for a bull of restitution to his see, the statute of *præmunire* was put in force against him, and he was confined for the rest of his life in Thorney Abbey, Cambridgeshire.

THE PRAGMATIC SANCTION, AND THE CONCORDAT.

The attempts that were made about this time to anticipate Christendom from the spiritual tyranny of the popes were not confined to one nation; and as a transaction which occurred in France probably had some influence upon the minds of the English, we may briefly advert to it here. The council of Basle met in the year 1431, pursuant to a decree of the council of Constance that perpetual general councils should meet every ten years whether the pope summoned them or not. This council abolished annates or first-fruits; wrested from the pope elections to vacant bishoprics and benfices, and restored them to chapters and local bishops, with confirmation by the metropolitan; condemned immediate appeals to the pope; and, chief of all, declared the council to be above the pope, that he was bound to submit to it, and that appeals lay to it from him. A contest arose with the pope, Eugenius IV., who summoned a council at Ferrara, in the year 1438, and excommunicated the members of the council of Basle, they in their turn deposing Eugenius from the popedom, and reviving the election of Amadeus, Duke of Savoy, under the title of Felix V., in the year 1439. The council of Basle addressed themselves for aid to Charles VII., king of France, who called a great assembly of nobility and Bishops at Bourges, who disapproved of deposing the pope, but reduced the decrees of the council of Basle into an edict, which was called *The Pragmatic Sanction*. For many years this law was observed in France, but it was occasionally suspended, and persevering efforts were made to get it repealed. At length, in the year 1516, Francis I. entered into an *agreement* called the *Concordat*, with Pope Leo X., whereby the king was to nominate to bishoprics within six months after a vacancy; if the pope disapproved, the king had three months more; if the king failed again, the pope was to provide one to the see; and all vacancies in the Court of Rome the pope was to fill up. Several attempts were made to recover the Pragmatic Sanction; but both the popes and the kings of France felt the advantages of the Concordat too sensibly to part with it.

ECCLESIASTICAL ABUSES.

A knowledge of the ecclesiastical abuses which tended to bring about the Reformation in England may have been gathered from the foregoing pages; but we will give a summary of them here. They are chiefly as follows:—The claims of the papacy to exclusive jurisdiction interference with the affairs of the kingdom, supremacy over the king, appointment to bishoprics and livings, annates, and the right of taxing the clergy; appeals to Rome; the prerogative of sanctuary; the luxury, covetousness, profligacy, and ignorance of the monks and clergy; the artifices and impudence of the mendicant friars; the abused doctrine of transubstantiation; the sale of indulgences; the worship of images; pilgrimages; dispensations, and papal interdicts and excommunications.

CHAPTER V.

From the Birth of Martin Luther till the Bible was set up in the Churches.—A. D. 1483-1541.

I. THE FIFTEENTH CENTURY.—Continued.

MARTIN LUTHER.

Luther was born of humble parents, at Eisleben, in Saxony, on the 10th of November, 1483. In early life he took upon himself the vows of an Augustinian friar, and was a devoted son of the Roman Church. At twenty-three years of age, he made a visit to Rome, where, it is said, his mind was awakened with respect to the purity of the faith, and practice of the Church to which he belonged. Upon his return he betook himself to the study of the Scriptures, with the help of Erasmus, and soon laid the foundation of that which has been called the distinctive doctrine of the Reformation—justification by free grace through faith in Christ only

II. THE SIXTEENTH CENTURY.

ACCESSION OF HENRY VIII.

Henry VIII. ascended the throne on the 22nd of April, 1509: Warham being at this time Archbishop of Canterbury, and Julius II., Pope of Rome. At this period, to a careless observer, few events seemed more remote than the violent disruption of those bonds which for ages had held England in connection with the Roman See. Henry was firmly attached to the Church of Rome, yet he soon undertook to restrict the privileges of the clergy; for in the year 1515, he put an end for one year to the exemption of the inferior orders of the clergy from being tried in the king's courts in cases of murder and burglary, which had existed for two centuries. This denial of immunity of Churchmen created violent sensation, being looked upon as an encroachment upon the privileges of the Church. Contests between the ecclesiastical and secular courts ensued, and were embittered by the death of Richard Hunne, a citizen of London, who, having been sued in the legate's court for a mortuary fee by his parish priest took out a writ of *præmunire* against the prosecutor. This incensed the clergy, and Hunne was imprisoned, on a charge of heresy, in the Lollard's tower, at St. Paul's. Shortly afterwards he was found suspended from the ceiling, with marks of violence upon his person, and a coronor's jury brought a verdict of murder against Dr. Horsy, the Bishop of London's Chancellor. Popular feeling was further exasperated by a sentence of heresy passed against the dead man, and the burning of his body in Smithfield, and the commencement by convocation of an action against Dr. Standish, to whose arguments against their immunities the clergy attributed the step of the coroner's jury. Upon an appeal to the king, it was determined that the convocation had incurred the penalty of a *præmunire*, and the members, with Wolsey at their head, went and begged the king's pardon on their knees. In answer to the suit of the clergy, the king made this memorable declaration:—"By the permission of God we are king of England; and the kings of England in times passed had never any superior but God only. Therefore, know you well that we will maintain the right of our crown."

ELECTION OF BISHOPS.

In the early part of the reign of Henry VIII., the manner of promotion to bishoprics and abbeys, was the same that had taken place ever since the investiture by the ring and staff was taken out of the hands of princes. Upon a vacancy, the king seized on all of the temporalities, and granted a license for an election, with a special recommendation of the person; which being returned, the royal assent was given, and it was sent to Rome that bulls might be expedited, and then the bishop-elect was consecrated; after that he came to the king, and renounced every clause in his bulls that was contrary to the king's prerogative, or to the law, and swore fealty; and then were the temporalities restored.

POPE LEO X.—INDULGENCIES.

Julius II., who was on the papal throne when Henry VIII. ascended that of England, disturbed Europe by scandalous wars. In the year 1513, he was succeeded by John de Medici, under the title of Leo X., a man of accomplishments and refinement, but also of unconquerable indolence and inordinate love of parade. The indulgence of his taste for luxury and magnificence, and the expense incurred in the erection of St. Peter's, drained the papal treasury; and in order to recruit it, he extended the traffic in indulgences. By these, the deluded people were taught to believe that they were absolved from all ecclesiastical censures, in whatever manner incurred, as well as from the penalties of all sins, how numerous soever they might be; so that whenever they might die, whether now or hereafter, the gates of punishment shut, and the gates of the Paradise of delight opened to them. Tetzel, a Dominican friar, was the principal agent for the disposal of these indulgences which were farmed; they were sold in the gross to the best bidders, and dispersed among the retail pedlars of pardons, who might be seen gambling in ale-houses, and staking the documents which professed to contain such mysterious powers. It was extravagance like this which first roused the indignation of the great German reformer, whose labors made themselves felt throughout Europe.

III. LUTHER, AND THE REFORMATION OF GERMANY.

While Luther was discharging the duties of his office, as Professor of Divinity in the University of Wittenberg, in the year 1517, he was roused to declaim against the infamous sale of indulgences conducted by Tetzel, the papal agent. Finding no warrant from the Scriptures for the practice, he determined openly and boldly to protest against the scandalous imposition practised upon his deluded countrymen. It does not appear that at this time he had any intention to throw off his allegiance to the Pope, but he drew up ninety-five propositions upon the abuse of indulgences which he was prepared to maintain against all opponents in public discussion at Wittenberg. He was now speedily engaged in controversy on every side, and upon further investigation he called in question the supremacy of the Roman Church and the authority of the pope. In the year 1520 he published a *Tract against the Popedom*, and soon afterwards his *Babylonish Captivity of the Church*. Open war was thus proclaimed, and on the 15th of June, in the same year, Leo excommunicated Luther, and condemned his books to be burnt. Luther returned measure for measure: he appealed from the pope to a general council, and on the 10th of December made a bonfire without the walls of Wittenberg, and threw into it decretals, canon-law, and bull, with his own hands. The news of what was passing in Germany soon made its way to England, and a hot persecution against the favorers of the doctrines of Luther was set on foot. Many were brought to the stake, among whom were six men and a woman, burnt at Coventry, for teaching their children the Creed, the Lord's Prayer, and Ten Commandments in the vulgar tongue. Frederick the Wise, elector of Saxony, and other princes in Germany, favored Luther, and prevailed upon the new emperor, Charles V., to have his cause publicly heard before the Diet of Worms, A. D. 1521.

NOTE.—When Luther was ordered to Worms, he was admonished beforehand of the fate which befell Huss, he replied that if they should kindle a fire all the way from Wittenberg to Worms that would reach to the sky, he would appear there, because he had been summoned; he would enter the mouth of behemoth between his great teeth to confess Christ, and let God order the result. Again, when he received, not far from the city of Worms, a warning from even his friend Spalatin against entering, he answered, "Were there as many devils in Worms as there are tiles on the roofs, I would still enter!" How the heart of Luther was stirred at that period, and yet how full of repose in God, appears from his prayer in Worms: "O God! O God! O Thou my God! Stand Thou by me, my God, against all the reason and the wisdom of the world. Do this. Thou must do it,—Thou alone. The cause is not mine, but thine. For myself, I have here no business nor aught to do with these great lords of the world. I would rather have peaceful days and live undisturbed. But the cause is thine, and it is righteous and everlasting. Help me, Thou true, eternal God. I lean upon no man. Vain and useless were it. Tottering is all that is fleshly or that savors of the flesh. O God! O God! .... Hearest Thou not, my God? Art Thou dead? No, Thou canst not die. Thou dost but hide Thyself. Hast Thou chosen me for this work? I ask Thee. Do not I know it! Aye, God has ordered it, for I never my life long thought to stand against such great lords. I never purposed it. O God! help me in the name of thy loved son, Jesus Christ, my defense, my buckler, aye, my strong fortress, through the power and strength of thine Holy Spirit! .... Lord, where art Thou? Thou, my God, where art Thou? Come! come! I am ready to lay down my life, patient as a lamb. For the cause is holy: it is thine own. I would not let Thee go,—no, nor yet for all eternity. That resolve is fixed in thy holy name. The world must leave me unconstrained in my conscience; and though it were thronged with devils, and this body, which is the work of thy hands and thy creature, be cast forth, trodden under foot, cut in pieces, thy word and Spirit remain good to me. And it is only the body! The soul is thine. It belongs to Thee. It will abide with Thee eternally. Amen! O God, help me. Amen!"

The God to whom Luther prayed was with Luther, and lent him courage to stand fast by the truth, and to present before emperor and empire words of confession which transcend many deeds of great heroes: "Unless, therefore, I am convinced through proofs from the Holy Scripture, am vanquished in a clear manner through the very passages which I have cited, and my conscience imprisoned thus by the Word of God, I neither can nor will retract anything. Here I stand. I can do nothing else. God help me. Amen!"

It was declared that Luther was an enemy of the Roman See, and thereupon was put under the ban of the empire as a heretic and schismatic; but Frederick concealed him in the castle of Wartburg for three quarters of a year, until the tyranny of the Diet was overpast. He worked hard in his retirement, employing himself in translating the Scriptures into the German language, laboring at his Commentary on the Epistle to the Galatians, and writing tracts against auricular confession, private masses, monastic vows, and celibacy of the clergy. Upon his release, he vigorously pursued the same career, and his doctrine spread rapidly. Hadrian VI. and Clement VII. demanded the punishment of himself and adherents, but could not prevail upon the German princes to proceed against them without the sanction of a general council.

NOTE.—About the year 1525, a long controversy was entered into by the German Reformers on the subject of the Eucharist: Luther maintained the doctrine of *consubstantiation*, namely, that in the Lord's Supper the body and blood of Christ are really present invisibly combined with the bread and wine, as fire is in heated iron, but only in the act of receiving the sacrament; but Zwingli asserted that there is nothing more than bread and wine, which elements are the figure and representation only of Christ's body and blood. A conference was held upon the subject at Marburg, which, however, broke up without coming to any accommodation. Meanwhile, opposition to the papacy gained ground, and two Diets were held at Spires, in Bavaria, to settle the religious disputes which prevailed. At the former, in the year 1526, the conflicting parties came to an arrangement which left the Lutheran States free to regulate their own ecclesiastical affairs, until the assembling of a general council. But this arrangement was set aside by the second Diet in 1629, in which all alterations and innovations in religion were prohibited by a majority of votes, until the promised general council should have met and promulgated its decrees. The Lutheran princes and states entered a *protest* against this edict, on account of which the name of *Protestants* was given to them. The term *Protestant*, therefore, originally signified one who protested against the edict of the Diet of Spire, in the year 1529.

DIET OF AUGSBURG.

In the year 1530 the Emperor Charles V. convened a Diet at Augsburg, with the intent of terminating the prevailing differences. The Lutheran party here presented their confession of faith, which has since been called *The Confession of Augsburg*. It was drawn up by Melanchton from *The Confession of Torgau*, and consisted of 28 chapters, of which 21 contained a brief summary of the opinion of the Reformers, and the rest pointed out the errors of Romanism. After an opposition to the Confession by Faber, Eckius and others, which was answered by Melanchton, several conferences were held to reconcile the contending parties; but the Diet, in the absence of many Saxon and Hessian princes, condemned the Protestants, and ordered them to submit themselves to the Pope; whereupon they confederated in their own defence in *The League of Smalcald*, and so obtained toleration from the emperor till the differences should be settled by a council. Various conferences and controversies afterwards took place, especially at Ratisbon, in 1541, when some points of difference were removed, and edicts against the Lutherans were suspended. Luther lived to see the opening of the famous council of Trent, which put him upon acting with more vigor and warmth against the Church of Rome, as foreseeing that measures were about to be taken for condemning his opinions. In short, he left no stone unturned to engage the Protestant princes to act against the council, continuing his exertions to that end until his death, which happened at Wittenberg, in February, 1546. After Luther's death, a formulary of faith and discipline, called *The Interim* (because it was only to be in force in the interim, *i. e. in the meantime* — till the decision of a general council), was obtruded upon the Protestants by the emperor, Charles V. In the year 1552, Maurice, Elector of Saxony, obtained advantages over the emperor, and concluded a peace with him at Passau, by which the religion and liberties of the Protestants were secured from further molestations. Thus Protestantism was settled in Germany.

REFORMERS.

In addition to Martin Luther the following were the prominent Reformers:—

GERMAN REFORMERS.

Melanchton.—Philip Melanchton, the greatest theologian of the Reformation and coadjutor of Luther, born 1497; taught at Tübingen University, 1514; called to Wittenberg 1418; published his "Loci Theologici," 1521; issued commentaries on the New Testament and parts of the Old; framed the Augsburg Confession, which gave a doctrinal basis to the Reformation, 1530; was long the trusted friend of Luther; died, 1560.

Erasmus.—Erasmus, of Rotterdom, born in 1467. In his satirical work, "Praise of Folly," he held up the abuses of Romanism to contempt, and contributed greatly to the preparation for the work of Luther. He revived the critical study of the Bible, especially of the New Testament, for the first time since the patristic period. He often vacillated between Rome and Wittenberg; general influence was favorable to the Reformation. Died 1536.

Princes.—Frederick the Wise, Elector of Saxony; his successor, John the steadfast; and Philip of Hesse. The number of knights and other noblemen who joined the Protestant cause rapidly increased. Many of them were personal friends of the reformatory theologians.

SWISS REFORMERS.

Zwingli.—Ulrich Zwingli, born in 1484, preached against the worship of the Virgin Mary at Einsiedeln, 1516; died, 1530. Bullinger was his successor.

Calvin.—John Calvin, born in France, 1509; fled because of his Protestant principles to Basle, 1534; published his "Institutes," 1536; lived in Geneva, 1536-1538; then banished, and resided in Strasburg, 1538-1541; returned to Geneva, 1541, and lived there until his death, 1564. Theodore Beza, born 1519, died 1601, was his successor in extending and building up the Swiss Reformation.

Farel.—William Farel, born, 1489; native of the French Alps; pioneer of the Reformation in Dauphiné and Switzerland; a most intrepid assailant of the Roman Catholic Church; died, 1565.

ORDER OF JESUITS.

The order of Jesus (Jesuits) was organized in 1540, by Ignatius Loyola, the first chief of the Order. Its objects were to support and promote the Roman Catholic religion by dividing and counteracting the growing Protestantism, and, by missionary labors to gain great territorial advantages. Francis Xavier was the greatest of Jesuit missionaries; under his directions the Jesuit missionaries were lying and deceiving the people at this time; adopting the idolatries of the heathen, substituting heathen traditions for the truth, and in many cases abandoning all pretence to Christianity and claiming to be ideal heathen devotees in order to secure an opportunity to administer baptism and the sacraments by craft and stealth, so as to thus secretly deceive the heathen into eternal life by the magical efficacy of outward rites.

The creed of the Order was: 1. The end sanctifies the means; 2. Mental reservation; 3. Distinction between philosophical and theological sins.

IV. THE REFORMATION IN ENGLAND.

Thomas Wolsey, the son of a butcher at Ipswich, was born in the year 1471. He was educated at Magdalene College, Oxford, where he obtained a fellowship. Having by ability, energy and good fortune, secured an introduction at court, he discharged a commission to the Emperor of Germany with such despatch and success that the old king, Henry VII., rewarded him with the deanery of Lincoln, a preferment which, together with that of royal almoner, he held on the accession of Henry VIII. Wolsey ingratiated himself with the young monarch by ministering to his pleasures, while he relieved him of the cares of business. In 1514 Henry made him Bishop of Tournay (his recent conquest in Flanders), then of Lincoln, and then Archbishop of York, all in one year. He also held the sees of Bath and Wells, Durham, and Winchester, successively, *in commendam*, together with the valuable abbacy of St. Alban's, and the Lord Chancellorship, in succession to Archbishop Warham; besides which he had pensions from the courts of Austria and France, and the surplus proceeds of the diocese of Worcester, after paying a moderate fixed income to his Italian incumbent. His opulence then became immense, and found vent in splendid buildings, a princely retinue, public magnificence, and private luxury. Having in 1515 been created Cardinal of St. Cecilia, and subsequently, A. D. 1519, legate, there was scarcely anything of professional rank or political power which was left him to desire. One object, to which his eyes had been long directed, still eluded his grasp — the popedom. After having maintained his unexampled elevation for fifteen years, the tide of fortune turned, when Wolsey was associated with Campegio in the legatine commission upon the subject of the king's divorce. He was ordered to deliver up the great seal, and to exchange the splendors of Whitehall and Hampton Court for the wretched accommodation of an unfurnished mansion at Esher. He died November 29, A. D. 1530.

SUBMISSION OF THE CLERGY.

Shortly after Wolsey's death the whole body of the clergy were placed under a *præmunire* for having acknowledged his legatine authority. An action was brought against them in the King's Bench, and the clergy of the southern province were glad to extricate themselves from their predicament by the payment of an enormous sum, £118,000, or about $560,000, granted to the king under the name of benevolence, in acknowledgement of his services to the Church and zeal against heresy. This payment was accompanied by a convocational recognition of his ecclesiastical supremacy. He was styled the protector and supreme head of the Church and clergy of England, with the saving clause, moved by Warham, "so far as is allowed by the law of Christ." The clergy of the northern province also voted a subsidy of £18,000, or about $56,000 ; but manifested considerable reluctance to acknowledge Henry supreme head of the Church. At length, however, the admission was made, Tonstall, Bishop of Durham, protesting against it. Thus, the Church's decision restored to the crown those powers which in Saxon times it had enjoyed, but which had long fallen into abeyance. These acts of convocation have since been known as the "snbmission of the clergy," that is, their submission to the prosecution under the *præmunire*, and not, as subsequently understood, to the acknowledgment of the royal supremacy as a new thing. The results of this submission were soon felt in an Act of Parliament, A. D. 1532, which abolished the payment of annates to the pope bulls of consecration, and provided also that, should the Pope refuse to consecrate in consequence, the ceremony should proceed under the authority of a royal mandate. And yet it does not appear that anything like religious innovation was contemplated, for a fierce persecution was begun against those who held what were opprobriously termed the "new opinions." The most remarkable victim was Thomas Bilney, of Trinity Hall, Cambridge, who was consigned to the flames at Norwich. Bayfield, a benedictine monk; Tewkesbury, a London tradesman; and Bainham, a member of the Temple, also suffered in Smithfield; and the body of William Tracy, of Toddington, Gloucestershire, was exhumed and burnt, for expressions in his will against testamentary bequests for soul masses.

HENRY MARRIES ANNE BOLEYN.

For two years Henry was attempting to get a divorce from Catharine, but in 1532, becoming tired of fruitless negotiations, he set the pope at defiance and married Anne Boleyn. Soon afterwards, Cranmer, who had been elevated to the primacy on the death of Warham, foreseeing the scandal that would arise if the king's first marriage was not formally annulled, summoned Catherine before his ecclesiastical court. Upon her refusal to obey, Cranmer pronounced her marriage with Henry null and void from the beginning, which was in accordance with the decision of the convocation. The pope first threatened, and subsequently, 1533, excommunicated Henry for adultery; his marriage with Catherine was pronounced valid and indissoluble; and he was ordered to live with her as a wife, under pain of ecclesiastical censures. This remarkable decision determined Henry at once to shake off the papal yoke.

RENUNCIATION OF PAPAL AUTHORITY.

Early in the year 1534 Parliament proceded to take measures which formally terminated the national connection with Rome. The law of Henry IV. for burning heretics was modified, and the power of bishops in convicting heretics was restrained. An act of the legislature confirmed the "submission of the clergy." Peter's-pence and all other pecuniary exactions of the court of Rome were abolished; and first-fruits, already taken from the pope, were given to the king. All dispensations and indulgencies, not contrary to the divine law, were henceforth to be granted by the archbishops. The sees of Worcester and Salisbury were declared vacant, because held by non-resident Italian incumbents. The marriage of Catherine was pronounced void and the off-spring illegitimate; and the succession of the crown was secured to the king's issue by the present queen. To that succession all were required to swear under the penalties of treason. Parliament also enacted a law (still in force) regulating the election and consecration of bishops.

By this law all bulls from Rome were condemned, and it was appointed that upon a vacancy the king should grant a *license to elect*, and should by a missive letter to the dean and chapter signify the name of the person he would have chosen. Within twelve days the dean and chapter were required to return an election of the person named by the king, under their seals. The bishop-elect was upon that to swear fealty, and a writ was to be issued out for his consecration in the usual manner. If the chapter refused to elect the person named, or the bishops to consecrate him when elected, they incurred the penalties of a *præmunire*.

Towards the close of the year an act was passed, declaring the king to be the "Supreme head on earth of the Church of England," which was appointed to be added to his other titles. By another act twenty-six suffragan, or *coadjutor*, bishops were appointed. The various branches of papal jurisdiction were by these measures removed. Convocation acquiesced in the proceedings, and pronounced that "the bishop of Rome has, in the Word of God, no greater jurisdiction in the realm of England than any other foreign bishop. One bishop only, the aged Fisher, refused to unite in this general decision of the Church; and thus the ordinary jurisdiction of the pope over England was regularly and lawfully suppressed.

PERSECUTION.

A young man of character and learning, named John Frith, was burnt for professing the very doctrine which Cranmer afterwards embraced, the denial of the change of the bread and wine in the Eucharist into any other substance. Many monks of the Charter-house suffered in the pope's cause, a party of them having been hanged at Tyburn. At the same time fourteen Anabaptists from abroad were burnt as heretics. Amid executions of less remarkable persons, Bishop Fisher was beheaded in June, 1535, and Sir Thomas Moore followed him to the scaffold two weeks later, for denying the king's supremacy. Upon the news of their death reaching Rome, the pope cited Henry to answer for it, and in case of refusal pronounced him excommunicate, placed his kingdom under an interdict, absolved his subjects from their allegiance, and commanded the bishops and clergy to quit the country.

FALL OF QUEEN ANNE BOLEYN.

Queen Anne Boleyn had uniformly exerted her influence with the king in favor of the Reformation, which excited the enmity of the popish party, although she grew in favor of the nation.

But it was felt, that as Catherine was now dead, all controversy might be set aside by the king's marriage with another, the legality of which marriage could not be questioned, nor the legitimacy of its issue. These reasons of State tallied with the king's affections, which were now transferred to lady Jane Seymour. Queen Anne was accused of adultery, and after a mockery of a trial condemned and executed, A. D. 1536. Next day Henry was married to Lady Jane, who died towards the close of 1538, two days after giving birth to a son, who was afterwards King Edward VI. Immediately upon the king's marriage with Lady Jane, a bill of succession was passed by Parliament, which confirmed sentences of divorce upon the two former marriages, and declared the issue by both to be illegitimate.

INSTRUCTIONS FOR A VISITATION OF THE MONASTERIES.

The monastic orders were the king's most persevering opponents in this rupture with Rome. They had ever been the creattures of the papacy: and now that the king's supremacy was established, their bulls from Rome were disregarded, and their trade in indulgencies ruined. So they thought it necessary for their own preservation to infuse into the people a dislike of the king's proceedings, and to embroil his affairs as much as possible. Henry, therefore, resolved to break the power of his enemies, and avail himself of their wealth to defend his kingdom without increased taxation. * Thomas Cromwell was made the king's vice-gerent in ecclesiastical matters, his authority being similar to that of a papal legate; and as a preliminary measure, it was determined that a visitation should be made of conventual establishments. Accordingly, commissioners were appointed, and the visitation began in October, 1535, and was completed in about ten weeks. The visitors were directed to inquire whether the houses had the full number according to their foundation, and if they performed divine worship at the appointed hours? How their heads were chosen? How their vows were observed? Whether they lived according to the severities of their orders? How the master and other officers did their duties? How their lands and revenues were managed? What hospitality was kept? How the enclosures of the nunneries were kept? Whether the nuns went abroad, or if men were permitted to come to them? How they employed their time, and what priests they had for their confessors?

DISSOLUTION OF THE LESSER MONASTERIES.

It is not improbable that the visitation was conducted with a view to make out a case against the monasteries. Yet an unfriendly scrutiny into a great number of conventual establishments, at a time when grossness of manner prevailed, would easily paint a very revolting picture, without any ingredient positively untrue. Such a picture undoubtedly was drawn by Henry's visitors. According to their report, not not only was property to a large amount discovered to have embezzled and and misapplied, and rules to be systematically violated, but the supposed abodes of contemplative piety, were found to be the scenes of violent passions and gross immoralities.

Many disgraceful impostures about relics and wonderful images were laid bare. The Rood of Grace, for instance, at Bexley, Kent, which hung its lip when a pilgrim offered silver, but shook its beard merely at an offering of gold, motions which the multitude attributed to divine power, was shown to be worked by wires. And at Hales, in Gloucestershire, the blood of Christ, which none in mortal sin could see, was a colored substance in a cunningly contrived vial, visible in one position and invisible in another. The smaller foundations were found to harbor the greatest amount of vice and fraud. Besides which, they were the houses of the friars, the most devoted of the pope's adherents and the busiest opponents of the king's supremacy; and the destruction of them would not greatly affect the powerful classes of society, for younger brothers were provided for in the wealthy abbey. Accordingly, in the year 1536, an act was passed, under which 376 monasteries, with incomes not exceeding £200 a-year, were suppressed, and their revenues, amounting to about £32,000 a-year, together with their plate and jewels, granted to the king, who secured the support of the nobility by bribing them with grants and sales at easy prices of the sequestered lands.

DEMOLITION OF BECKET'S SHRINE.

The shrine of Thomas à Becket, who was slain by some of the officious servants of Henry II., in the cathedral of Canterbury, was the richest and most famous in England. In 1537 Henry seized upon his treasures; and the remains of the prelate were disinterred, arraigned of treason, and dispersed or burnt. This vengeance upon the remains of one so mixed up with papal triumph may possibly be accounted for by the fact, that at this period the pope was openly encouraging the rebellion of Henry's subjects, having published his bulls of excommunications and deposition, which had been suspended since the death of Fisher and Moore. He also endeavored to inflame the kings of Scotland and France against Henry; and Cardinal Pole was despatched to the Netherlands with invitations to the continental sovereigns to aid the rebellion in England. Pole's conduct so enraged Henry, that the Countess of Salisbury, the Cardinal's venerable mother, was ordered to the scaffold, the victim for her son's offence.

DISSOLUTION OF THE LARGER MONASTERIES.

Not long after the fall of the lesser monasteries, a visitation of the larger houses was set on foot, to inquire into the purity, sincerity, and, what was more questionable still, the loyalty of the inmates. The royal designs being very evident, not a few conventual superiors bowed to the coming storm, and made a voluntary cession as the best way of escaping difficulties and securing comfortable annuities. The abbots of Tewkesbury and Bury St. Edmund's were of this class; but the abbots of Reading, Colchester, and Glastonbury, having refused to surrender, paid the forfeit with their lives. Other resignations were obtained by promises of pensions or threats of exposure. The number of monasteries suppressed was 555; and in the year 1539 an act was passed which gave the king the control of their revenues, amounting to nearly £160,000 a year. In the following year, a statute, dissolving that half-military, half monastic fraternity, the Knights Hospitallers of St. John of Jerusalem, extinguished the last remnant of English monachism.

THE SIX ARTICLES.

The supremacy and the suppression of the monasteries having been carried, the king almost deserted the cause in which he had been so actively engaged, and for the rest of his reign surrendered himself for the most part into the hands of Romanist advisors. Cromwell, the political agent of the Reformation, fell into disgrace, for the part he had taken in promoting the king's marriage with a German princess, Ann of Cleves, and subsequently suffered as a traitor. Gardiner, Bishop of Winchester, the most astute politician of his time, succeeded him in the king's favor; and against such a man as Gardiner, the single-hearted primate could exert but little influence over the conduct of Henry. Under the influence of the new advisors of the crown, in May, 1539, the same Parliament which confirmed the dissolution of the larger monasteries decreed that royal proclamations should have the force of law, and proceeded to pass, on the motion of the Duke of Norfolk, an act to establish the following "Six Articles" of faith :—

(1) The doctrine of transubstantiation, or real presence.

(2) Communion in one kind; that is, the giving of the cup to the clergy only, and not to the laity.

(3) The celibacy of clergy.

(4) The perpetual obligation of vows of chastity.

(5) The efficacy of private masses.

(6) The necessity of auricular confession.

The penalty for the breach of the first of these articles was burning as a heretic; and of any of the others, hanging as a felon. Against five lashes of this "whip with six strings," Cranmer argued with so much temper and ability that he won the applause even of his opponents. But the king supported the sanguinary bill in person, and the enemies of the Reformation succeeded in getting it passed. The effect of the act of "Six Articles" was soon visible. Latimer, now Bishop of Worcester, and Shaxton, now Bishop of Salisbury, were driven from their bishoprics; and Cranmer himself was only rescued from its full operation by the interference of the king. Many of the clergy were forced to separate from their wives: Cranmer was amongst the number, and he sent his wife and children into Germany. The commissioners appointed to carry the act into execution erected themselves into a kind of inquisition-general and brought within the compass of it everything that savored of what they called heresy. The prisons of London were therefore gorged with culprits, and Smithfield witnessed many of those dreadful scenes which have made its name so famous.

Among the victims were Barnes, a divine of some Character, whose real offence was an attack upon a sermon by Gardiner, and his Lutheran views of justification, and two other clergymen, Garrat and Jerome. Soon after their execution, a boy of fifteen, named Mekin, was burnt for heresy, although he recanted at the stake, through the influence of the infamous

7

Bonner, Bishop of London. At a subseqent period, a young gentlewoman of distinction, named Ann Askew, or Ayscough, heroically endured the rack without a groan; and declining to retract her denial of the doctrine of transubstantiation, was carried, while yet suffering from the cruelties inflicted on her frame, and burnt in Smithfield, together with several others animated by a like spirit. Indeed, the executions were so numerous that it has been said more men were put to death in this reign than afterwards suffered in that of Mary. In the years 1540 and 1544 the severities of the act of the "Six Articles" were mitigated through the instrumentality of Cranmer; and the penalties in some cases were commuted into confiscation of property; and no accusation was to be made upon a sermon after forty days, nor upon words spoken after a year. In 1547 the act itself was revoked.

CHAPTER VI.

From the time the Bible was set up in the Churches till James I. ascended the throne.—A. D. 1541-1603.

I. THE SIXTEENTH CENTURY.—Continued.

THE BIBLE SET UP IN THE CHURCHES.

Cranmer's Great Bible appeared in 1540. It was a corrected edition of Matthew's Bible and obtained Cranmer's name because he wrote a preface to it. This Bible had the royal sanction, and in 1541 every parish was bound, under heavy penalties, to provide a copy to be set up in the church, so that all might come and read it.

QUEEN CATHARINE PARR.

After his divorce from Anne of Cleves, the king married Catharine Howard, a niece of the Duke of Norfolk, who was condemned and executed for treason. In July, 1543, he married his sixth and last wife, Catharine Parr, widow of Lord Latimer. This event was looked upon with pleasure by the Reformers; for Catharine favored their doctrines, and was a woman of some learning and a religious frame of mind. She was herself the writer of a religious treatise, *The Lamention of a Sinner*, and procured the translation into English of Erasmus' Commentary on the New Testament, which was afterwards set up in Churches together with the Bible.

Formularies of faith. — Besides the setting up in churches of the Bible and the commentary of Erasmus, other books of religious instruction were put forth on authority in Henry's reign. In the year 1536, convocation impressed its sanction upon "Ten Articles," entitled *Articles devised by the King's Highness Majesty to stablish Christian quietness and unity amongst us.* These were probably compiled by Cranmer, though ostensibly emanating from the crown. Five of the Articles related to doctrines, and five to ceremonies. The former were—

(1) That the Holy Scriptures and the three Creeds are the basis and summary of a true Christian faith.

(2) That baptism is absolutely necessary, as well to children as to adults.

(3) That penance consists of contrition, confession and reformation, and is neccessary to salvation.

(4) That the body and blood of Christ are really present in the elements at the eucharist.

(5) That justification is the remission of sin and reconciliation to God, by the merits of Christ; and that good works follow after justification.

The latter were—

(1) That images are useful as remembrancers, but are not objects of worship.

(2) That saints are to be honored as in the enjoyment of glory, and as furthering our prayers.

(3) That saints may be invoked as intercessors, and their holydays observed.

(4) That ceremonies are to be observed for the sake of their mystical signification, and as conducive to devotion.

(5) That prayers for the dead are good and useful; but the efficacy of papal pardon, and soul masses offered at particular localities, is negatived.

Upon the preceding Articles was founded the *Institution of a Christian Man*, commonly known as *The Bishops' Book*, from its having come forth with the sanction of all prelates, which was published A. D. 1537. It consisted of an exposition of the Apostels' creed, the seven sacraments (matrimony, baptism, confirmation, penance, the Lord's supper, holy orders, and extreme unction), the Paternoster, and the Ave Maria; in addition to this the Articles on justification and purgatory were set forth at the end, the others having been inserted in the body of the work under their respective heads. The doctrinal errors of Rome were for the most part retained in the *Bishops' Book*, and yet it was clear that the Reformers had done something. The corruption of man was strongly asserted; consequently the virtues of a redemption were vindicated, and placed in a position from which the dogma of merit had depressed them: and superstitious attention to trifles of ceremonial, and the dishonest substitution in sermons of fables, and inventions of men for the Scriptures, were rebuked.

THE KING'S PRIME.

The King's Prime was a collection of prayers and devotions, with expository and instructive matter, intended for all ages, but more especially for the young. It was published in 1543.

DEATH OF MARTIN LUTHER.

Luther went (1546), at the desire of the counts of Mansfield, to Eisleben, arriving January 23d. He had first preached in Wittenberg (January 17th), with forebodings of his end, exhorting his people to constancy in the faith and against apostasy. Reaching his former place of abode, he said, "If I can but reconcile my loved lords, the counts of Mansfield, here in Eisleben, to each other, I will go home, lay me down in my coffin, and give my body to the worms to devour." He preached in Eisleben four times (January 31st, February 2nd, 7th, and 12th). One prayer and hope had often been uttered by him. As he says, "I have with great earnestness prayed God, and do now pray him every day, that He would hinder the design of the foe, and suffer no war to come upon Germany in my life-time; and I am assured that God has certainly heard this my prayer, and I know that while I live there will be no war in Germany." His desire was granted him. There was fulfilled in him the saying, "The righteous is taken away from the evil to come." He fell ill on the 17th of February. Feeling his end approaching, he prayed, "O my father, God and Father of our Lord Jesus Christ, Thou God of all Comfort, I thank Thee that Thou hast revealed to me thy dear Son Jesus Christ, in whom I believe, whom I preached and confessed, whom I have loved and praised, whom the evil pope and all the ungodly dishonor, persecute, and revile. I pray Thee, my Lord Jesus Christ, that my soul may be dear to Thee. O heavenly Father, if it be so that I must leave this body and be torn away from this life, yet know I surely that I shall ever abide with Thee, and none shall pluck me out of thine hand." He repeated the words, "God so loved the world that he gave his Son," and "He that is our God is the God of salvation, and unto God the Lord belong the issues from death." He added thrice, "Into thine hand I commit my spirit. Thou hast redeemed me, O Lord God of truth." And when Justus Jonas said to him, "Reverend Father, will you die steadfast, clinging to Christ and to the doctrine which you have so constantly preached?" he answered emphatically,

"Yes!" Soon after he fell asleep, on the morning of February 18th. Let my soul die the death of this righteous man, and my last end be like his!

DEATH OF HENRY VIII.

Henry VIII. died on the 28th of January, 1547, in the 56th year of his age, and the 38th year of his reign. On his deathbed, at his own request, he received the consolations of religion from Cranmer. During the whole of his reign the Church remained in appearance Romish. He was, humanly speaking, the instrument whereby the three great barriers to improvement, the papacy, monasticism, and spiritual ignorance, were broken down. He was, however, only an unintentional pioneer of the Reformation. The dissemination of the Bible in the vulgar tongue, aided by the passions and arbitrary character of the king, may in some measure account for the facility with which the pope's authority was overthrown. But at Henry's death, there was not unanimity even among the Reformers themselves. The seven sacraments, transubstantiation, communion in one kind, auricular confession, the celibacy of the clergy, and other ancient forms which were still retained in the Church, formed subjects of controversy among the advocates of the Reformation.

ACCESSION OF EDWARD VI.

Edward VI., Henry's son by his third wife, Lady Jane Seymour, was born on the 12th of October, 1547, and succeeded his father before he had completed his tenth year. He was a child of more than usual promise; and as his tutors, Coxe and Cheke, had imbibed Protestant principles, all the personal weight, which one so young could have, was given to the cause of the Reformation. It was a favorable circumstance for that cause that Gardiner, its greatest enemy, had so fallen in the late king's favor, that he was omitted from the list of sixteen executors nominated to act as a council to the young prince, and maintain the succession to the crown as devised in the event of his decease without issue. Edward was crowned on the 20th February, by Cranmer; upon which a general amnesty, released from confinement a pious band of confessors, which, daily augmented by returning exiles, went forth to disseminate the principles of Scriptural Christianity. The Duke of Norfolk and Cardinal Pole were excepted from the amnesty.

IMAGES—VISITATION OF THE CLERGY.

A few weeks after Edward's accession, Ridley, afterwards Bishop of Rochester, and then Bishop of London, preached in the Chapel Royal against the use of images as helps to devotion, and the lustral water of paganism, naturalized among Romanists under the name of holy water. About the same time the cause of images received a further blow in the failure of a memorial against the curate and churchwardens of St. Martin's, London, for having supplied their places with texts of Scripture.

Gardiner defended the use of images, which he distinguished from idols, arguing that the latter only were condemned, as the representations of a false God, whereas the former were representations of a true God; and that as words, by means of the ear, begat devotion, so might images by means of the eye. The Protector, probably under Cranmer's direction, replied that the bishops made a pretended abuse of the Scriptures the ground for taking them away from the people, although they were commanded to be offered to all; which argument held much more strongly against images, that were forbidden by God's law. Yet the Protector complained of the intemperate zeal of certain persons, who had broken down images without authority. This was the first step in this reign towards a reformation; and it was speedily followed by a royal mandate, directing curates to dissuade their flocks from pilgrimages and image-worship, and to take down such images, pictures, &c., as had been used for superstitious purposes. Commissioners were also appointed, at the instance of Cranmer, by an order in council, to visit all England, and inquire into the discipline and religious practices of both clergy and people.

FIRST BOOK OF HOMILIES.

One of the first measures taken by Cranmer to lay the foundation of a Scriptural theology in men's minds was the publication of a "Book of Homilies," or plain discourses adapted to the capacities of the people. There was a necessity for this step in consequence of the lack of educated preachers, and the Homilies were composed with a view to being read to their congregations by incumbents who were unable to write discourses of their own. The "First book of Homilies" was set forth in the first year of Edward's reign. It consisted of twelve discourses, composed, it is thought, by Cranmer and his associates, among whom Ridley and Latimer probably rendered most valuable service. Its object seems to have been the general improvement of the people in religious knowledge, and a confirmation of them against some of the less prominent, but vital prejudices derived from a popish education. The volume proves that at this period, whatever was thought of transubstantiation and the mass, the doctrine of justification through the merits of Christ, by faith, was clearly apprehended. In addition to the publication of Homilies, *Erasmus' Paraphrase*, already translated into English, was ordered to be set up in every Church, and the Lord's-day to be religiously observed. Gardiner and Bonner interposed obstacles to these proceedings (the former objecting especially to the Homily on salvation, as excluding charity from the work of justification), and were imprisoned for their refractoriness in the Fleet.

REPEAL OF THE SIX ARTICLES.

The close of the year 1547 witnessed the repeal of the "Six Articles," and of all the statutes that made anything treason or felony in the late reign which was not so before, as well as of the acts against the Lollards, and that which gave the king's proclamation the authority of law.

CRANMER'S CATECHISM.

In the year 1548 Cranmer put forth an English catechism, or *A Short Instruction to Christian Religion for the Singular profit of Children and Young People*. Originally written in German it was put into Latin by Justus Jonas, and translated thence into English under the direction of Cranmer, whose name was prefixed to it. It was an exposition of the ten commandments, the creed, the Lord's prayer, and the sacraments. This catechism marks the progress of Cranmer's mind. The commandments are still arranged after the Romish usage (the second being omitted or incorporated with the first, and the tenth divided into two); three sacraments are insisted on; and the real presence in the Lutheran sense (consubstantiation) is maintained.

BOOK OF COMMON PRAYER.

A commission of twelve divines, with Cranmer at their head, was appointed to prepare an English liturgy. Gardiner was excluded from the commission; but Bonner was one of the consulting bishops. Being, however, opposed to all change, his opinion had probably very little weight. Ridley, Rowland Taylor, Dr. Coxe, and the Bishops of Lincoln (Holbeach), Ely (Goodrich), and St. David's (Farrar), were probably Craumer's most efficient associates. They met at Windsor, and the sources from which they drew the matter of the "First Book of Common Prayer" were the existing service-books, correcting what was objectionable in doctrine, removing what was offensive in taste, and improving all by happiness of expression. The reformed liturgy was first used on the festival of Whit-Sunday, June 10, 1549. The Lady Mary forbade the introduction of the Prayer-book into her establishment, and continued the use of the old Latin mass, alleging that during the king's minority no alteration could legally be made in the arrangements left by her father. About this time England was convulsed by turbulence among the peasantry, especially in the west.

NOTE. — Heterodox opinions of an opposite character were introduced this year by certain persons from Germany, who denied the right of infants to baptism and the personal Deity of the Saviour and of the Holy Spirit; advocated community of goods, polygamy, and divorce, rejected oaths and magistracy; and professed other dangerous opinions, for which the Reformation was held responsible by its enemies. But its friends rebutted this charge by the questionable course of persecuting the holders of the above opinions; and Joan Bocher, or Joan of Kent, and a Dutchman named George Van Parre, were consigned to the flames on a charge of heresy.

In 1550 six bishops and six other divines were empowered to prepare a new form of ordination, in harmony with the principles upon which the liturgy had been reconstructed. The new ordinal, while it expunged minor grades, distinctly recognized the three orders of bishops, priests, and deacons, as having subsisted from Apostolic times. Imposition of hands was retained; but a number of rites, as the anointing, the giving of sacred vessels, and various minutiæ of no very great antiquity, were discarded, and replaced by the delivery of a Bible, significant of a chief duty of a Christian minister. Heath, Bishop of Worcester, refused his assent to the alterations, and was consequently sent to prison — so ill-understood in those days were the principles of toleration.

SACERDOTAL VESTMENTS.—ALTARS.

Bishop Hooper entertained an invincible repugnance to sacerdotal vestments, identified, in his opinion, with exploded superstitions, and positively refused to wear the episcopal dress, which still continued to be of scarlet, as having been invented with the object of investing the celebration of mass with a character of magnificence far from accordant with the restored simplicity of worship. Cranmer and Ridley, as well as Bucer and Martyr, tried in vain to induce Hooper to forego, for the sake of unity and peace, his determination to dispense with the customary habits at his consecration. He continued inflexible, and it was not till after an imprisonment in the Fleet that a compromise was effected, Hooper stipulating that he should wear the disliked habits only on important public occasions. In the same year Hooper was probably instrumental in procuring the removal of altars, and the substitution of tables. In preaching before the Court, he said "it would be well to change altars into tables, according to Christ's first institution; for, so long as altars remain, both ignorant people, and ignorant or disposed priests, will ever be dreaming of sacrifice." Ridley ordered the removal of altars in his diocese of London, while Day enforced their preservation in that of Chichester. An order in council put an end to this disagreement, by directing that altars should be removed, and a table set up instead in some convenient part of the chancel, to serve for the ministration of the blessed communion. The Bishop of Chichester still refusing compliance, was imprisoned, and ultimately deprived.

REVISION OF THE BOOK OF COMMON PRAYER.

The Prayer-book of 1548 was constructed upon the cautious principle of rejecting nothing from the ancient forms of devotion unless repugnant to the sacred volume. But this principle of non-repugnance to Scripture was deemed insufficient to exclude error: nothing but what was immediately derived therefrom, it was thought, had any right to appear in a directory of public devotion. A careful review was therefore made of the whole, for the purpose of getting rid of objectionable Romish usages, by Cranmer, and two learned foreigners, Peter Martyr and Martin Bucer, who had been installed, through Cranmer's influence in the chairs of theology at Oxford and Cambridge. The revised liturgy was first used by Bishop Ridley on the festival of All Saints, 1552.

ARTICLES OF RELIGION.

Although the attention of the Reformers had been chiefly directed to the reformation of the offices of the Church, the importance of framing Articles of Religion, which should speak with authority the opinions of the Church, and secure uniformity amongst her teachers had not been overlooked. Cranmer had desired that a conference of Protestant divines might agree upon a united confession of faith, and had consulted Melancthon and Calvin on the subject. But perceiving little prospect that his object would be accomplished, he felt it imperative that England should no longer remain unprovided with a formal exposition of her Church's tenets. In obedience, therefore, to his sovereign's command, Cranmer began in 1551 to draw up Articles "for preserving and maintaining peace and unity of doctrine in the Church." They were forty-two in number, and were printed in Latin and English in the year 1553, under the title of "The Articles agreed upon by the Bishops and other godly men, in the last Convocation at London, in the year of our Lord 1552, for to root out the discord of opinions, and stablish the agreement of true religion; likewise published by the king's majesty's authority, 1553." During his labors, Cranmer appears to have consulted Ridley and other divines; and from the identity of expression, especially on the subjects of free-will, original sin, and justification, it is evident that they had before them the confession of Augsburg—so that the spirit of the Articles is Lutheran, not Calvinistic. This was Cranmer's last public work in the English Reformation.

DEATH OF EDWARD.

Scarcely was the finishing stroke put to the doctrinal fabric of the Reformed Church of England by the royal signature, when the king, who had taken so deep an interest in its progress, was called away. Edward's constitution began to decline towards the close of 1552. Having completed the political arrangements which proposed to supersede the Lady Mary by his cousin Lady Jane Grey, Northumberland's daughter-in-law, the young king breathed his last, on the 6th of July, 1553, in the sixteenth year of his age, and the seventh of his important reign.

THE REIGN OF MARY.

An attempt to place Lady Jane Grey upon the throne at Edward's death was productive only of increased stability to the crown of Mary. The day of Mary's accession was one of gloomy presage to all who desired the permanence of what had been accomplished, but she allayed rising apprehensions, by assuring magistracy of London that she would force no one's religion. This assurance, however, had scarcely passed her lips, when it became evident that she would not rest until Romanism had been re-established. The deposed prelates were liberated and restored to their sees. Gardiner, again Bishop of Winchester, was made Lord Chancellor; and Northumberland died on the scaffold, abjuring his former faith with most abject hypocrisy. Several bishops were expelled from their sees, and replaced by others constituted by the pope. Before another month had elapsed Ridley, Hooper, Latimer, Coxe, Rogers, Bradford, Judge Hales, Chief Justice Montagu, and others, were in confinement either for preaching without a license, or declaring Edward's laws to be still in force or general encouragement of the Reformation. Cranmer, too, was ordered to keep his house, and hold himself in readiness to answer the summons of the council; he was soon afterwards committed to the Tower for a declaration in writing against Mary's proceedings, as also for his participation in Lady Jane Grey's attempt, and so commenced an imprisonment from which no discharge awaited him save through the flames of martyrdom.

RECONCILIATION WITH ROME.

In July, 1554, the Queen was married to Philip of Spain, and an insurrection, under Sir Thomas Wyatt and the Duke of Suffolk, ensued, for the match was distasteful to the nation. Many of the nobility were compromised in this insurrection, and numbers of them, including Wyatt and Suffolk, forfeited their lives. Lady Jane Grey and her husband were also executed; and even the Princess Elizabeth was arrested on suspicion of being concerned in the late rising. Strengthened by the discomfiture of rebellion, Mary condemned the severest proceedings against the favorers of the Reformation. A new parliament was summoned, and orders were issued to sheriffs to take care that such only were chosen to serve in it as were of the "wise, grave, and Catholic sort." Having secured a parliament to her mind, Mary received Cardinal Pole, who was appointed papal legate, with great respect; and parliament sought and obtained the pope's absolution to the English nation for the schism of which it had been guilty. All statutes passed against the Roman see were abrogated, and the title "Supreme Head of the Church" was disowned, as having never of right belonged to the crown. The marriage of the clergy was an object of special attack, and many who had separated from their wives were deprived of their livings. The use of the Latin service was restored, and directions given for the repression of heresy. It is supposed that sixteen vacancies occurred on this episcopal bench in consequence of the orders and injunctions put forth at this time; and of course these were soon filled by zealous Romanists. An immense number of priests, variously estimated at from one-fourth to three-fourths of the whole, were also deprived. In short, a very savage persecution assailed those who rejected the papal supremacy. Through the zeal of the "bloody Bonner" the fires of Smithfield blazed continually. According to Short 270, and according to Burnett, 284 persons perished in the flames, and multitudes were driven into exile.

DISTINGUISHED MARIAN MARTYRS.

A detailed account of that noble army of martyrs who suffered in the reign of Mary comes not within the scope of this small work; it must be sought for in the pages of John Fox. But we may here briefly advert to a few of the more distinguished. — *John Rogers*, the supposed translator of "Matthew's Bible," Vicar of St. Sepulchre, London, was the first victim whose blood cemented England's alliance with the pope. He was burnt in Smithfield on the 4th February, 1555.—Next day *Hooper*, Bishop of Gloucester, was removed from London to that city, where he was burnt on the 9th of February, for denying the corporal presence, and refusing to separate from his wife. The wood was green, and he suffered prolonged agonies with admirable constancy.—On the same day *Rowland Taylor* was burnt at Hadleigh, Suffolk, of which place he was rector.—*Bishop Farrar* suffered in the market-place of Carmarthen, on the 30th of March. — *John Bradford*, committed to prison on the charge of exciting a disturbance, which he had in fact assisted to allay, when Bonner's chaplain attacked the measures of Edward's reign at St. Paul's, was brought to the stake in Smithfield, after fruitless attempts to make him recant, on the 1st of July.—The history of Cranmer, Latimer, and Ridley is a common one.—*Thomas Cranmer* was born at Aslacton, Nottinghamshire, in 1489. He was educated at Jesus College Cambridge, where he obtained a fellowship, which he vacated by marriage. His wife, however, died in a short time, when he was re-elected Fellow of Jesus College, and charged by the University with the examination of candidates for the Divinity degree. When the plague visited Cambridge in 1529, he retired with two of his pupils to the house of their father at Waltham Cross, and was there introduced to Henry VIII. In 1533 he succeeded Warham as Archbishop of Canterbury. *Hugh Latimer*, born at Thurcaston, Leicestershire, in 1470, was a disciple of Bilney's in Cambridge; upon Anne Boleyn's elevation to the throne, he was appointed one of her chaplains, and afterwards raised to the bishopric of Worcester, which he resigned on the passing of the "Six Articles," and never could be induced to resume it. *Nicholas Ridley* was born at Wilmontswick, Northumberland, in 1500, and in 1522 graduated at Pembroke College, Cambridge, of which he subsequently became master. He became chaplain to Henry VIII., by whom he was promoted to the see of Rochester in 1547, and he was finally elevated to the see of London by Edward VI. in 1550. Cranmer, Latimer, and Ridley were imprisoned on the accession of Mary on a charge of treason, for having favored the cause of Lady Grey; but this charge was eventually commuted into one of heresy. After remaining some months in the tower, where they read together the New Testament, and found therein no encouragement to the doctrine of transubstantiation, they were removed to Oxford, to attend a public disputation with the delegates of the university, under the presidency of Weston, Dean of Westminster, upon the following questions, which form the substance of four articles put forth by convocation as a test of heresy:—

(1) Whether the natural body of Christ and his natural blood are really present in the sacrament?

(2) Whether after consecration there remains any other substance than the body of Christ?

(3) Whether in the mass there is a sacrifice and propitiation for the sins both of the living and the dead?

Cranmer disputed on the 16th of April, 1554, Ridley on the 17th, and Latimer on the 18th. An impartial hearing was out of the question; taunts, hisses, and personal insults supplied to the dominant party the place of argument. "It was one of those cowardly contests," says Professor Blunt, "'ubi tu cædis, ego vapulo tantum; where one strikes, and the other must be content to be smitten." The glory of the contest rested with Ridley, rather than the other two; throughout he adhered to one line of argument, explaining all the authorities advanced against him of the spiritul presence only. Two days after the last disputation, all three were brought to St. Mary's Church, and declining to recant were condemned as heretics. But their execution was delayed, in the case of Latimer and Ridley for eighteen months, and in that of Cranmer for five months longer still, which time they employed in promoting the glory of God and the good of their generation. Indeed, the sentence had been pronounced without authority, for there was no statute in force which made a denial of transubstantiation penal. It was requisite, therefore, that proceedings should commence anew; accordingly on the 12th of September, 1555, Cranmer appeared at St. Mary's before Bishop Brooks, of Gloucester, sitting as a papal delegate, and at the close of the proceedings was cited to appear at Rome within eighty days, this formality being necessary before a metropolitan could be condemned. Latimer and Ridley were cited before papal delegates on the 30th of September; and continuing inflexible, were condemned and pronounced excommunicate. On the 15th of October, they were formally degraded; and on the following morning conducted to the place of suffering in the town ditch, opposite Balliol College, where they were burnt, Latimer exclaiming when the lighted faggot was applied, "Be of good comfort, Master Ridley, and play the man: we shall this day, by God's grace, light such a candle in England as, I trust, shall never be put out." Meanwhile the last sands of Cranmer were rapidly running out. Long before the eighty days allowed for his appearance at Rome had expired, letters arrived authorizing his condemnation and deliverance to the secular arm; and on the 14th of December he was degraded by Bonner and Thirlby with all that brutality of insult which none but a Bonner could have displayed towards one to whom he was indebted for his original elevation. Had Cranmer been led at once to the stake, he would doubtless have crowned a consistent testimony by an honorable martyrdom. But his enemies endeavored, too successfully, to prevail upon him to sign a recantation. All at once an unusual interest was manifested in him by the University authorities; he was invited from his gloomy prison of Bocardo to the mansion of the Dean of Christchurch, where hopes were held out that the Queen only desired such a retraction as might justify her in extending to him the clemency she earnestly desired to exercise. To these things were added the entreaties of his former friend, Thirlby; and the consequence was that his resolution gave way, and he signed various documents retracting all he had taught contrary to the doctrines and authority of the Roman see. All this while preparations were going on for his execution, and, with a duplicity which is a fit consummation of the whole, he was kept in ignorance of his intended fate until almost the hour of his immolation. On the 21st of March, 1556, the very day of his executon, his eyes were opened by a visit from Dr. Cole, Provost of Eaton, who furnished him with the usual preliminary to an execution in the shape of fifteen crowns to give to the poor. He was informed that his recantation must be read in public, and was conducted to St. Mary's Church, where, after a sermon from Cole, his confession was to be made. At the conclusion of the sermon Cranmer rose, and having prayed and addressed some words of exhortation to the people, pronounced a summary of his faith, utterly renouncing the recantations into which he had been deceived, "as things written with my hand contrary to the truth which I thought in my heart, and written for fear of death, and to save my life, if it might be. And forasmuch as my hand offended, writing contrary to my heart, my hand shall first be punished therefore; for, may I come to to the fire, it shall be first burned." After renouncing the pope, and all his false doctrine—not forgetting the papistical doctrine of Eucharist—his voice was drowned in the reproaches of the bystanders. Upon this he was hurried to the place already consecrated to the memory of Latimer and Ridley, amidst the insults of the friars, who kept continually reminding him of his recantation. When the flames began to ascend, stretching forth his right hand, he held it therein, ofttimes repeating, " This unworthy right hand, this unworthy right hand!" so long as his voice would suffer him; and using the words of Stephen, " Lord Jesus receive my spirit," in the greatness of the flame he gave up the ghost. Thus perished Cranmer, nobly redeeming in death the irresolution that clouded the latter hours of his life.

DEATH OF MARY.

The leading Reformers had either perished or gone into exile, when the unhappy Queen ended a reign of continued disaster on the 17th of November, 1558. Cardinal Pole, her chief religious adviser, followed her to her grave within sixteen hours of her own decease. She suffered the barbarity of Romanism to be so displayed that moderate people revolted from a religion which spake of peace, but shed blood like water upon the earth. Hence, bonfires were lighted in the streets before Mary was cold, and tables spread for merry-making in honor of her successor.

THE REIGN OF ELIZABETH.

On Mary's demise, her half-sister, Elizabeth, succeeded amid the acclamations of all except the bigots, who felt that the reign of terror was closed. She had conformed to Romanism in the late reign, when non-compliance might have endangered her life. But her anti-Romanist feelings were indicated on her accession by the refusal of her hand to Bonner; by the gratification with which she received a Bible on her procession through London; and by the appointment of eight friends of the Reformation upon her council. Yet she resolved to proceed with circumspection in her dealings with a divided people. For instance, at her coronation, on the 15th of January, 1559, she partook of the mass, Romanism being then the religion of the country; in order to avoid controversy she silenced all *preachers*, whether Protestant or Romanist, until the meeting of Parliament; she at first refused, but at last conceded, the marriage of the clergy.

THE ACT OF SUPREMACY.

Parliament met ten days after the Queen's coronation, and one of its earliest proceedings was the passing an act for restoring first-fruits and tenths to the crown. The laws which had formerly been made with the concurrence of the Church in the reigns of Henry and Edward were also restored. The Act of Supremacy was also passed; it imposed upon persons taking office, or ecclesiastical preferment, that they would respect the ecclesiastical supremacy which the constitution vested in the Crown: but the title of "Head of the Church," which had caused many disputes, was omitted, and that of "Supreme Governor" substituted, as less liable to be misunderstood. Most of the parochial clergy took the oath of supremacy; but many deans, heads of colleges, and prebendaries refused it, and were consequently deprived. The whole episcopal bench, with the exception of Kitchin, Bishop of Llandaff, also refused the oath, and fourteen bishops were therefore ejected from their sees. The leniency shown to the ejected bishops contrasted strongly with the measure dealt out to the Protestant prelates deprived, degraded, and burnt, under Mary's administration. With the exception of two or three, who were imprisoned for threatening the Queen with excommunication, not a shadow of harshness was shown against them. Even the cruel Bonner, instead of receiving the due reward of his atrocities, was permitted to live luxuriously in a prison, which proved to him a refuge from the rage of an indignant people.

CONSECRATION OF PARKER.

It became a matter of immediate necessity to replenish the ranks of an episcopacy reduced by the numerous deprivations consequent upon the Act of Supremacy. Matthew Parker, who had been Master of Corpus Christi College, Cambridge, and Dean of Lincoln, but was deprived in the reign of Mary, was consecrated Archbishop of Canterbury on the 17th of

December, 1559, by Barlow (Bishop of Bath and Wells), Scory (Bishop of Chichester), Coverdale (Bishop of Exeter), and Hodgkins (Suffragan of Bedford), according to King Edward's ordinal.

JEWEL'S CHALLENGE AND APOLOGY.

John Jewel, Bishop of Salisbury, was an exile in Mary's reign. In a sermon at Paul's cross, after the accession of Elizabeth, he strenuously denied the *antiquity* of Romish tenets, and subsequently challenged the most learned of that party, in no less than twenty-seven points of difference, commencing with private masses, and ending with the position that "ignorance is the mother of devotion," to produce any one sufficient sentence out of any ancient father, or general council, or from Holy Scripture, or example from the primitive Church, declarative of the Romish view. This was followed by his celebrated *Apology for the Church of England*, which received the sanction of convocation in 1562, and had more effect in confirming the Reformation than any other book ever published. It repels in the outset the calumnies with which the Reformation had been assailed as heretical and schismatical, showing that they had rather returned to the state of the primitive Church than occasioned a schism, and that the innovation with which they were charged was only a rejection of modern errors introduced by the Church of Rome.

RISE OF PURITANISM.

As the English Reformation revealed the full spirit of popery, so it made us acquainted with another spirit of a very different nature and origin, viz,, that of Protestant dissent. The Puritan separation (so named from its supporters professing greater *purity* of divine worship) dates from the year 1570. It took its rise from the exiles in Mary's reign, who having acquired during their foreign residence a taste for the doctrines and discipline of Calvin and Zwingli, upon their return sought to reform the Church upon a Genevan model. They declaimed against her as infected with popish errors and superstitions, objecting to episcopacy, set forms of prayer, surplices, instrumental music, chanting, the ring in marriage, bowing at the name of Jesus,* &c. They were opposed and punished by

8

Elizabeth, and by Archbishops Whitgift and Bancroft; and "the judicious Hooker," in his immortal exposition of the principles of the Reformation, happily convicted them of their destructive opinions.

PERSECUTION OF THE HUGUENOTS.

The Massacre of French Protestants (Huguenots) on St. Bartholomeu's night, occured at Paris, in 1572. 70,000 people were killed. There were great rejoicings and public thanksgiving at Rome. This led to the edict of Nantes in 1598, securing to the French Protestants the full exercise of their religion.

THE PROPHESYINGS.

In Elizabeth's reign, clerical meetings were held in several dioceses, under the patronage of the bishops, for the discussion of theology and the expounding of Scripture. These meetings were termed *Prophesyings*, from St. Paul's expression (1 Cor. xiv. 31), "Ye may all *prophesy*, one by one, that all may learn, and all may be comforted." They excited the Queen's displeasure, as calculated to encourage too much freedom of religious discu sion, and as tending probably to raise questions touching her supremacy; she, therefore, ordered that they should be suppressed. She also desired that the number of preachers should be diminished. Grindal, who succeeded Parker in the primacy, A. D. 1576, conceived that the *Prophesyings* might, under proper regulations, both tend to edify the people, and to stimulate the less earnest of the clergy to Scriptural research; and he considered that the number of preachers, instead of being diminished, ought rather to be greatly increased. He ventured, therefore, to expostulate with the Queen, who therefore deprived for a time, and never again admitted him to her favor. The *Prophesyings* were suppressed; and Grindal was nominally restored to his see several years afterwards.

THE THREE ARTICLES.

Whitgift, Master of Trinity College, Cambridge, succeeded Grindal in the primacy in 1583. He was a consistent opponent of Puritanism, and in his diocese of Worcester he had furthered the Queen's views as regarded the *Prophesyings*. One of his earliest acts was the issue of three articles, afterwards embodied in the 36th canon, which the clergy were required to subscribe, namely, (1) an acknowledgment of the royal supremacy; (2) a declaration that the book of Common Prayer containeth nothing contrary to the Scripture, with an engagement to use no other form of Divine Service; and (3) the confirmity of the thirty-nine articles to the Word of God. Following this up, he required the administration of the oath *ex officio* to suspected clergymen. These proceedings excited great opposition, and many clergymen who refused to comply were suspended. A great deal of violence was shown, and scurrilous attacks upon episcopacy were published, one of which, under the title of *Martin Marprelate*, made a great noise, and led to the imprisonment of Cartwright.

THE COUNCIL OF TRENT.

This was the most celebrated of the assemblies regarded by the Roman Catholic Church as ecumenical or general, and the great repository of all the doctrinal judgements of that communion on the chief points at issue with the reformers of the 16th century. Very early in his conflict with pope Leo X., Luther had appealed from the pope to a general council; and after the failure of the first attempts at an adjustment of the controversies, a general desire grew up in the church for the convocation of a general council, in which the true sense of the church upon the controversies which had been raised might be finally and decretorially settled. Another, and, to many, a still more pressing motive for desiring a council, was the wish to bring about the reform of the alleged abuses as well of the court of Rome as of the domestic discipline and government of local churches, to which the movement of the reformers was in part at least ascribed. But the measures for convoking a council were long delayed, owing partly, it has been alleged, to the intrigues of the party who were interested in the maintenance of those profitable abuses, and especially of the officials of the Roman court, including the cardinals, and even the popes themselves; but partly also to the jealousies, and even the actual conflicts, which took place between Charles V. and the king of France whose joint action was absolutely indispensable to the success of any ecclesiastical assembly. It was not till the pontificate of Paul III. (1534-49) that the design assumed a practical character. One of the great difficulties regarded the place of meeting. In these discussions much time was lost; and, without entering into detail, it will suffice to say that the assemby did not actually meet till Dec. 13th, 1545, when 4 archbishops, 22 bishops, 5 generals of orders, and the representatives of the emperor and the king of the Romans, assembled at Trent, a city of Tyrol. The number of prelates afterward increased. The pope was represented by three legates, who presided in his name—cardinals del Monte, Cervino, and Pole. The first three sessions were devoted to preliminaries. It was not till the fourth session (April, 1546) that the really important work of the council began. It was decided, after much disputation, that the doctrinal questions and the question of Reformation should both be proceeded with simultaneously. Accordingly, the discussions on both subjects were continued through the fourth, fifth, sixth, and seventh sessions, in all which matters of great moment were decided ; when a division between the pope and the emperor, who, by the victory of Mühlberg, had become all powerful in the empire, made the former desirous to transfer the council to some place beyond the reach of Charles's arbitrary dictation. The appearance of the plague at Trent furnished a ground for removal and in the eighth session a decree was passed (March 11th, 1547) transferring the council to Bologna.

This translation was opposed by the bishops who were in the imperial interest, and the division which ensued had the effect of suspending all practical action. Meanwhile, Paul III. died. Julius III. who had, as cardinal de Monte, presided as legate in the council, took measures for its resumption at Trent, where it again assembled May 1st, 1551. The sessions 9 to 12, held partly at Bologna, partly at Trent, were spent in discussions regarding the suspension and removal; but in the 13th session the real work of the assembly was renewed, and was continued slowly, but with great care, till the 16th session, when, on account of the apprehended insecurity of Trent, the passes of the Tyrol having fallen into the hands of Maurice of Saxony, the sittings were again suspended for two years.

But the suspension was destined to continue for no less than nine years. Julius III. died in 1555, and was followed rapidly to the grave by his successor (who had also been his fellow-legate in the council as cardinal Cervino), Marcellus II. The pontificate of Paul IV. (1555–59) was a very troubled one, as well on account of internal difficulties as owing to the abdication of Charles V.; nor was it till the accession of Pius IV. (1559–65) that the fathers were again brought together to the number of 102, under the presidency of cardinal Gonzaga, re-opening their deliberations with the 17th session. All the succeeding sessions were devoted to matters of the highest importance — communion under one kind; the sacrifice of the mass; the sacrament of orders, and the nature and origin of the grades of the hierarchy, marriage, and the many questions connected therewith. These grave discussions occupied the sessions 17 to 24, and lasted till Nov. 11th, 1563. Much anxiety was expressed on the part of many bishops to draw the council to a conclusion, in order that they might be enabled to return to their sees in a time so critical; and accordingly, as the preliminary discussions regarding most of the remaining questions had already taken place, decrees were prepared in special congregations comprising almost all the remaining subjects of controversy, as purgatory, invocation of saints, images, relics, and indulgences. Several other matters, rather of detail than of doctrinal principle, were referred to the pope, to be by him examined and arranged; and on the 3rd and 4th of Dec., 1563, these important decrees were finally read, approved, and subscribed by the members of the assembly, consisting of 4 cardinal legates, 2 other cardinals, 25 archbishops, 168 bishops, 7 abbots, 7 generals of orders, 39 proxies of bishops—making in all 252.

These decrees were confirmed, Jan. 10th, 1564, by Pius IV., who had drawn up, based upon them in conjunction with the creeds previously in use, a profession of faith known under his name. The doctrinal decrees of the council were received at once throughout the western church, a fact which it is necessary to note, as the question as to the reception of the decrees of doctrine has sometimes been confounded with that regarding the decrees of reformation or discipline. As to the latter, delays and reservations took place. The first country to receive the decrees of the council as a whole was the republic of Venice. France accepted the disciplinary decrees only piecemeal and at intervals.

EXTENSION OF PROTESTANTISM.

To this century belongs the honor of planting the first Proestant church on the soil of the new world. Under the advice of Coligny and Calvin, the Huguenots, tormented beyond endurance in Europe, made a settlement at the mouth of the Amazon river in 1554, and founded a church which maintained itself until 1567, when it was broken up by the Romish leader of the Portugiese settlement at Rio de Janeiro.

Gustavus Vasa, the first Protestant king of Sweden, a pronounced Lutheran, not only established the Lutheran church as the state church of Sweden, but carried on a mission to Lapland, which was continued by his grandson, Gustavus Adolphus. Vasa caused the translation of the Scriptures and hymn books for both Lapps and Finns, and opened schools. The result was a wide diffusion of both intelligence and Protestantism among both races.

Some beginnings of Protestant Christianity were made in North America in the last part of the century. Sir Walter Raleigh and others began settlements in the middle Atlantic region, but these were more colonization than missionary in character.

CHAPTER VII.

From the accession of James I. till the present time.
A. D. 1603–1884.

Elizabeth closed a long and prosperous reign on March 24, 1603, and was succeeded by James VI. of Scotland, called James I. of England.

THE HAMPTON COURT CONFERENCE.

The accession of James I. excited the hopes of those who desired ecclesiastical changes, and a petition, called, from the number of names attached to it, the *Millenary Petition*, was drawn up, praying for an amendment as regarded:

(1) *The Church Service.* They objected to the cross in baptism; interrogatories to infants; confirmation; baptism by women; the cap and surplice; the ring in marriage; bowing at the name of Jesus; communion without previous examination; the priest and absolution; the reading of the Apocrypha.

(2) *Church Ministers.* They prayed that none but preaching ministers be admitted to the ministry; that non-residency be not permitted; that subscription be not urged, except only to the articles of religion and the king's supremacy, according to law.

(3) *Church Administration.* They desired that commendams and pluralities be abolished; that impropriations annexed to bishoprics and colleges be demised only to preaching incumbents; and that lay impropriations be charged with the maintenance of a preacher.

(4) *Church Discipline.* They objected to excommunication or censure by a layman, or without the pastor's consent; certain abuses in the ecclesiastical courts; the too frequent use of the oath *ex officio*, by which men were forced to accuse themselves; the incautious granting of marriage licenses without bans being asked.

In answer to this petition, James appointed a conference between the Puritans and the Church party, which was held at Hampton Court on January 14, 1603, and the two following days. The king himself acted as moderator: the established system was represented by Archbishop Whitgift, and Bishops Bancroft (London), Matthew (Durham), Bilson (Winchester), &c.; and the other side by Drs. Reynolds and Sparke from Oxford, and Mr. Knewstubbs and Mr. Chatterton from Cambridge. The alterations agreed to were considerable. They consisted principally of the omissions of two portions of the Apocrypha; viz., the close of the History of Susanna, and the story of Bel and the Dragon; an enlargement of the Catechism by questions on the sacraments; the insertion in the liturgy of prayers and thanksgiving for special occasions; and the forbidding of private baptism by women, or by any, except lawful ministers.

SYNOD OF DORT.

In the reign of James, religious dissensions broke out amongst the Dutch, in consequence of what were deemed the schismatical proceedings of their theological professor at Leyden, James Arminius (formerly pastor at Amsterdam), who considered election, so far as it respected individuals, to be altogether contingent upon human conduct, and divine grace to be neither *irresistible* when offered, nor *indefectible* when possessed. With the view of settling these disputes between the Arminians and the Calvinists, the Synod of Dordrecht, or Dort, was convened in 1619, the king sending five divines to represent the English Church. The Calvinistic party prevailed, and it was determined:

(1) That election is an absolute and irreversible decree of God to save a certain portion of the human race, while the rest are left to perish in their sins.
(2) That the sacrifice of Christ is *sufficient* for the whole world, but *efficient* only for the elect.
(3) That the human will, faculties, and affections, are wholly depraved, and naturally incapable of originating any spiritual act.
(4) That the saving grace of the Holy Spirit is infallibly efficacious in the elect.
(5) That all such persons regenerate and freed from the dominion, though not from the presence of sin, shall be certainly preserved.

These propositions formed the subject of what has been called, from its consisting of five articles, the *Quinquarticular Controversy*, and which has not even yet terminated.

ARCHBISHOP LAUD.

James I. died at Theobalds, March 27, 1625, and was succeeded by Charles I. From the day of Charles's accession, Laud was the virtual director of the English Church, the aggrandizement of which was one of the great schemes of his life. His father was a clothier at Reading, and he was born there in 1573. He was educated at Oxford, where he made himself obnoxious to the Calvinistic party, at the head of which was George Abbot, afterwards Archbishop of Canterbury. He became successively President of St. John's College, Dean of Gloucester, Bishop of St. David's, Bishop of Bath and Wells, Bishop of London, and finally, Archbishop of Canterbury, upon the disgrace of Abbot in 1633. One of his earliest acts as Primate was republication of the *Book of Sports*, first issued by James I. in 1618, which authorized certain games and pastimes on the Sabbath. Laud raised against himself numerous enemies by his irritability of temper, and his extreme notions of the royal prerogative and the supremacy of the Church, and he was at length impeached by the Long Parliament; committed to the tower in 1641; and beheaded on the 10th of January, 1645.

THE STAR CHAMBER.

During the primacy of Laud, new vigor was infused into the high Commission, established in the reign of Elizabeth for the trial of ecclesiastical offences, whose criminal prosecutions were conducted in the more ancient Court of Star Chamber. This Court was originally the Privy Council itself, sitting in a room, the ceiling of which was ornamented with stars. It was remodelled by **Henry VII.** for the cognizance of official misdemeanors, without the assistance of a jury; but its jurisdiction now extended to the enforcement of all royal proclamations, and the punishment of all libels against authority. In the reign of Charles I., it became so arbitrary and tyrannical that it was abolished. Upon this, Parliament began to interfere in matters of religion.

NOTE. — One of the first acts of Parliament was the appointment of a committee for the removal of *scandulous* (i. e. loyal) *ministers*. This was followed by a more summary and systematic ejectment of the loyal clergy. By a subsequent ordinance episcopacy was abolished, and the Liturgy superseded by a Directory, drawn up by a body of Presbyterian and Independent Divines. By another ordinance, it was directed, that all monuments of superstition and idolatry, such as crosses, crucifixes, &c., and all representations of any angel or saint, be removed, defaced, and demolished; and that all copes, vestments, roods and surplices be taken away. And of the scenes of devastation that were then enacted, most of the cathedrals and finer ecclesiastical buildings yet retain the memorials. At Oxford, as they refused compliance with the changes, the heads, and most of the members of the University, were summarily ejected. A similar process had already taken place at Cambridge, where the parliamentary proposals were rejected with almost equal equanimity.

FIFTH MONARCHY MEN.

A fanatical sect appeared during Cromwell's Protectorate, who considered his assumption of power as an earnest of the foundation of the *Fifth Monarchy*, which should succeed to the Assyrian, Persian, Grecian, and Roman, and in which Jesus Christ should reign with the Saints (*i. e.*, themselves) on earth for the space of a thousand years. Upon the restoration of the royal family, a party of these enthusiasts, headed by one Venner, made a desperate insurrection in the streets of London, which was put down with the slaughter of a great number of them.

THE SAVOY CONFERENCE.

Upon the restoration of Charles II., the Acts of the Long Parliament being deemed void, episcopacy was restored and the liturgy came again into use. The Presbyterian divines, who, in an interview with Charles at the Hague, had been led to expect such a modification of episcopacy as no reasonable Presbyterian could object to, took alarm at this, and presented a petition to the king, to which the bishops replied; and soon afterwards the king published a declaration, in which concessions in matters of discipline were made, and a commission promised for the revision of the liturgy. The promised *Conference* commenced its sittings at the residence of the Bishop of London, in the *Savoy*, on April 15, 1661. There were twelve bishops on one side, and twelve Presbyterian ministers on the other, with nine assistants on each side. Baxter on the part of the presbyterians, prepared a list of objections and an entirely new form of prayer; and after discussion, spread over many weeks, the Presbyterians specified the following eight points as actually *sinful*:—

(1) That no minister might baptize without using the cross.

(2) That none might officiate who scrupled the surplice.

(3) That none might communicate who declined to kneel.

(4) That ministers were forced to pronounce all baptized children regenerate by the Holy Ghost, whether they be the offspring of Christians or not.

(5) That ministers are obliged to deliver the communion to the unfit.

(6) That ministers are obliged to absolve the unfit, and in absolute terms.

(7) That they are forced to give thanks for all whom they bury as those whom God hath in mercy taken to himself.

(8) That none may be a preacher, that dare not subscribe that there is nothing in the Common Prayer, Ordination service, and 39 Articles, that is contrary to the Word of God.

The commission expired on July 24, 1661, and the parties had come to no agreement except with regard to some small concessions in the liturgy.

FINAL REVISION OF THE LITURGY.

The concessions made at the Savoy Conference were laid before the convocation, and the following principal alterations were sanctioned:—

(1) The *Authorized Version of the Bible* to be used, except in the Ten Commandments, the Psalms, and the sentences in the Communion service.

(2) The five prayers for the Sovereign, royal family, clergy, and people, with St. Chrysostom's and the Benediction, at the end of the *Litany*, were transferred to the *Morning* and *Evening Services*.

(3) The second prayer for fine weather, and those for the *Ember-weeks*, for the *Parliament*, and for *All Conditions of Men*, with the *General Thanksgiving*, and that *For Restoring Public Peace at Home*, were added.

(4) Some new *Collects* were introduced, changes made in others, and "Church" substituted for "Congregation."

(5) The *Exhortation*, in giving notice of the Communion, was ordered to be read on the Sunday or some holiday before its administration, and persons were required to give notice of their intention to communicate: the admonition against *Transubstantiation* was also introduced.

(6) *The Baptismal Service for those of Riper Years*; the *Form of prayer to be used at Sea*; and the last five prayers in the *Visitation of the Sick*, were added, and the absolution of the sick was left to the curate's discretion.

(7) The consent of the curate was required before *Confirmation*, but the bishop might dispense with it; and *Confirmation* was not absolutely necessary for admission to the *Communion*.

(8) In the *Churching of Women* the *Psalms* were changed, and the service might be read from the desk.

(9) *New-married* people were exhorted, but not required to receive the Lord's Supper.

(10) The *Font* to be placed at the discretion of the ordinary.

(11) In the *Catechism*, the words "Because they promise them both by their sureties," &c., were substituted for "Yes, they do perform them by their sureties who promise and vow them in their names," &c.

(12) The absolution was ordered to be pronounced by the priest alone.

(13) The clause respecting departed Saints was added to the Church Militant prayer.

(14) In the service for baptism, the clause "Sanctify this water to the mystical washing away of sin" was introduced, and that affirming the certain salvation of all baptized infants was annexed.

SPREAD OF PROTESTANTISM.

As early as 1613 the Dutch settlements in the new world brought Protestantism into the region of Manhattan Island and northward upon the Hudson; and the landing of the Pilgrims in New England planted the same faith there in 1620. In 1634 the colony of Maryland gave formal tolerance to both Protestant and Romish worship.

There was no special design of missions in these settlements in the new world, but they were of the utmost significance as related to the future missionary work of the Protestant churches.

This century was marked by the struggles of Protestantism to secure independence and recognition. Protestantism, as soon as it had fairly asserted its rights to be, began to break up into a great number of parties representing various phases of theological thought. Parties, and sections or bodies of people in different sections of Europe, one after another secured religious liberty to a great or less degree, and began to assume distinctive names. The English State church sprang up and began to take a shape. About the middle of the century, 1641, there was organized in England a "Society for the Propagation of the Gospel in Foreign Lands." Again, in 1649, the English Parliament chartered the "Society for Propagating the Gospel in New England," while in New England itself, a new activity had sprung up in the work of Eliot for the Indians of Massachusetts, which work led to other similar work by Mayhews,

Brainerd and others, and never ceased from that day to this, being carried on by various different bodies at different times and in different places, by varying agencies.

Several migrations to the New World occurred toward the close of the century. Considerable numbers from the reformed churches of Holland settled about New York; 2,000 colonists took possessions, of Pennsylvania the first year of its founding by Wm. Penn, the Quaker; a large number — 3,000 or more— of Presbyterians were forcibly transported from Scotland and sold as slaves in Virginia; the Huguenots from France found a home in New York and in South Carolina; great numbers of Lutherans continued to remove to America for years.

In 1691 the Christian Faith Society began work, and in 1698 the Society for Promoting Christian Knowledge was organized —both in England. Danish missions in India had already begun, but were carried on by individuals and sustained by private contributions.

With the opening of the eighteenth century the religous world showed a more hopeful and active condition, Protestantism was an assured fact. There was to be yet much tribulation for those who dared to worship God in their own way, but their extermination was recognized as impossible. The various branches of Protestantism were becoming well organized, self-possessed and more or less aggressive. And this very subdivision into sects was an advantage both to a pure faith and to the spread of the Gospel. Libertines or Spiritualists; Anabaptists; Sacramentarians; Schwenckfeldians; Socinians; Anti-Trinitarians; Mennonites; Independents; Mystics; Baptists of various stripes; Ranters; Seekers; Familists; Unitarians; Quakers; and others previous to the eighteenth century, had all done something either directly or indirectly, to strengthen Protestantism, and increase its aggressiveness.

In 1701 the Society for Propagating the Gospel in Foreign Parts was organized in England, and took up the greater part of the colonial work of the Society for Promoting Christian Knowledge, and operated in North America, West Indies, Russia, and the Levant.

In 1714 the king of Denmark established the Royal College

of Missions at Copenhagen, where large numbers of men were trained for the foreign missionary work.

The Moravians who had been dispersed and scattered in 1648 from Bohemia and Moravia, now began to gather new strength. From a safe retreat in England their history was written and the order of ordained clergy maintained and perpetuated. A remnant left at Fulneck in Moravia were obliged to leave in 1690, and found refuge with Count Zinzendorf, in Herrnhut. By 1733 they had become so strong that they opened a mission to Greenland, and thus began one of the most wonderful of all modern missions. In 1736 they began among the Hottentots of Africa; in 1737 in Guiana; 1739 in Algiers; 1740 in Ceylon, and among the gypsies of Europe, and the Jews at Amsterdam.

In 1731 Hans Egede, the Norwegian, made his famous journey to Greenland, two years in advance of the Moravian movement in the same direction. In 1714 there was a society for missions in Norway organized, which, though a home missionary society, did much to rouse missionary zeal.

Among the notable movements in the early part of this century was that internal revival of practical piety within the church itself in England, under the Wesleys and others; and a similar movement in New England under Whitefield and others, who, together, were instrumental in the "Great Awakening" of 1720 — in Great Britain and America. Undoubtedly the rise and vigor of nineteenth century missions in America is due to this revival of practical piety under Whitefield, Edwards, the Tennants and others.

It is worth noting that in 1754 was organized Moor's Indian Charity School, at Hanover, N. H., which was the germ of Dartmouth College; and in 1762 the Society for Christian Knowledge among Indians was incorporated by the Massachusetts legislature.

A different, but no less hopeful phase of the religious activity of the close of this century is seen in the origin of the ragged schools in England under Raikes, and the organization of a Sunday school society in 1785, which was the forerunner of several Sunday school unions in different parts of Great Britian.

In 1792 the Particular Baptists of England organized the Baptist Missionary Society, and subsequently sent Carey to India, in 1793, established a mission at Sierra Leone in 1792.

In 1795 also the London Missionary Society was organized by the English Congregationalists and Presbyterians, and began work at Tahiti, In the same year appeared the Glasgow Missionary Society, for the benefit of the Kaffir tribes in Africa. In 1796 arose the Edinburgh Missionary Society for work in Jamaica; it afterward became the Scottish Missionary Society, and later transferred its work to other societies. In 1797 the Rotterdam Missionary Society was founded and became in 1818 the "Netherlands" Society.

The religious Tract Society was organized at London in 1799, for the distribution of religious literature in all lands.

Besides these there were a number of home missionary organizatios among the English and continental churches.

In America the Missionary Society of Connecticut 1799; the Massachusetts Missionary Society in 1799; and several other State societies in New England were laying the foundations for the American Home Missionary Society and the American Board of Commissioners for Foreign Missions, which were the pioneer general missionary societies for enlisting national interest and effort in the two lines of home and foreign work.

These movements showed that the Reformation had not been in vain. The church of Christ, so long enthralled by priestly tyranny and widespread ignorance, was beginning to awake and shake herself loose from her bonds. The revival of a purer faith naturally led to more earnest works. The church began to remember her great commission, and to set herself about fulfilling it. True, only beginnings were made; but they were beginnings, and some of them were not only notable in themselves, but became beginnings of heroic and fruitful labors in years following.

WESLEY, AND ENGLISH METHODISM.

In 1739 there was a general religious decline in England. French frivolity and native Deism prevailed in the upper classes; the lower were vicious and neglected. The clergy were ungodly. Reform took place through the Wesleyan movement. John Wesley, the founder of Methodism, was born at Epworth, England, in 1703. He began his studies at Oxford in 1729, and became a Fellow there; labored among the poor and neglected, and was at the head of a small society of pious young men, called, in contempt, the "Holy Club," of which his brother Charles and George Whitefield were members. He went to Georgia as a missionary in 1735, and returned in two years to England: was converted through the influence of Jacob Böhler, a Moravian, in 1738, and founded the first Methodist society in the following year. The societies multiplied rapidly, though the use of the churches of the Establishment was denied John Wesley, Whitefield, and their coadjutors. John Wesley died in 1791. While both the brothers wrote many hymns, Charles Wesley's chief contribution to the growth of Methodism lay in this department. He was born 1708, and died 1788. George Whitefield, was born 1714, died 1770. John Fletcher, was born 1729, died 1785. The last was the leading controversial writer in early Methodist history. Joseph Benson, preacher and commentator, born 1748 died 1821. Adam Clarke, the chief commentator and linguist of Methodism, born 1762, died 1832. Richard Watson, born 1781, and died in 1833. He was the author of the doctrinal standard of Methodism, the "Theological Institutes."

THE VIRGINIA COLONY.—PROTESTANT EPISCOPAL CHURCH.

The founding of the Virginia Colony on James River by Captain John Smith and other members of the Established Church of England was in 1607. The Rev. Robert Hunt is said to have preached the first sermon in English on the American continent. The colony was divided into eleven parishes in 1619. The Church of England form of worship prevailed in the colonies south of New England.

First General Convention of the Protestant Episcopal Church of the United States was held in Philadelphia, representing seven States, 1785. *Prayer Book*, published 1786, omitted the Nicene and Athanasian Creeds, the descent into hell of the *credo*, absolution, and baptismal regeneration, and made bishops amenable to the lower clergy. The objections of the

English bishops led to a restoration of nearly all the expunged parts, except the Athanasian Creed and absolution in visitation of the sick. By special act of Parliament the English bishops were enabled to ordain William White, Samuel Provost, and Dr. Griffith, February 4, 1787.

REFORMED EPISCOPAL CHURCH.

Bishop Cummins seceded from the Protestant Episcopal Church in 1873, and organization in New York, Dec. 2, 1873,) the Reformed Episcopal Church. Subsequently Dr. Cheney ordained him to the Episcopacy. Reformed Episcopal Churches have been established in various parts of our own country and the British dominions.

The principles of the Reformed Episcopal Church are: Belief in the Bible as rule of faith and practice; in the Apostles' and Nicene Creeds; in the two sacraments of Baptism and Lord's Supper, in the Thirty-nine Articles of the Church of England; in the retention of the Episcopacy, not as necessary, but as ancient and desirable; in a Book of Common Prayer free from all Romanizing elements; in extemporaneous prayer; in the non-regenerative power of baptism; and in the non-observance of saints' days.

THE PURITANS IN AMERICA.—CONGREGATIONALISM.

The Puritan pilgrims in the Mayflower landed at Plymouth, Massachusetts, in 1620. Though coming from England originally, they had sailed last from Holland. Another colony and church was organized in 1629 at Salem; in 1630 another church at Charlestown; colonies from Massachusetts Bay in Connecticut in 1635; adoption of the Cambridge Platform in 1648. The Congregational Church took its rise from the Puritan colonists. During the last century it was confined chiefly to New England.

REFORMED CHURCH.

Until recently, called the Reformed Protestant Dutch Church. First settlement in New Netherlands of members of this church from Holland was in 1623. Arrival of the first preacher, Jonas Michaelius, in 1628. Great embarrassment of the organization for many years because of the use of the Dutch language in worship, and connection of the church in this country with the parent church in Holland. Independent organization effected in 1771, through the agency of Rev. Dr. J. H. Livingston. Secession in 1822 of churches on the score of laxity in doctrine and discipline. The seceders took the name of the True Reformed Dutch Church, and now number less than twenty congregations.

THE BAPTISTS.

Founding of the First Baptist Church in America by Roger Williams, at Providence, Rhode Island, in 1639. Early progress very slow, because of the Baptists being persecuted both North and South. They enjoyed no freedom except in Rhode Island, Pennsylvania, and Delaware. The American Revolution marked the beginning of great progress, which has been general and steady ever since. Minor Baptist Churches:—Anti-Mission; Free-will; Seventh-Day; Church of God, or Winebrennarians; Disciples of Christ, or Campbellites; Tunkers; Mennonites.

GERMAN REFORMED CHURCH.

Organization of the church, 1741. First missionaries sent out by the church in Holland; and the German Reformed Church remained in connection with the Dutch Church until 1792. It was made up, in the early part of its history, of emigrants from the Palatinate Switzerland. It is mainly distinguished from the Reformed (Dutch) and the French Reformed churches by its use of the German language.

THE LUTHERAN CHURCH.

The first Lutherans in this country were in New York; the first pastor, Rev. Jacob Fabricius, 1669; the first church was a log hut, 1671. The second settlement was on the Delaware, 1676. Rev. H. M. Muhlenberg arrived from Germany in 1742. He became the leader of the Lutherans in this country. First Synod, was held in 1748. The Lutherans are now most numerous in Pennsylvania and Ohio, and are very vigorous. The Lutherans are divided into;—1. The strict old Lutherans; 2. The moderate Lutherans of the Pennsylvania Synod; and 3. The Evangelical Lutherans.

THE PRESBYTERIANS.

From 1660 to 1685 three thousand persons of Presbyterian faith were transported, as slaves, during the persecutions in Scotland, to the American colonies. By 1688 many Presbyterian immigrants, settled in Eastern Pennsylvania. Rev.

Francis M'Kenzie was the first Presbyterian minister in America. The Presbytery of Philadelphia was organized in 1706. First General Assembly (John Rodgers, Moderator) of the Presbyterian Church of the United States, 1789. There were then 188 Presbyterian ministers, and 419 churches. An attempt was made to unite all Presbyterians but failed. There was a division of the Presbyterian Church in 1838. In St. Louis, Missouri, 1866, attempt made to initiate the reunion of the Presbyterian Church, (Old and New School). Consummation of the re-union was effected in 1870.

THE METHODISTS IN AMERICA.

The first Methodist Society established in New York by Barbara Heck, Philip Embury, and Captain Webb, 1766; Methodist church built in John street, 1768; Richard Boardman and Joseph Pilmore arrived from England, 1769. Boardman labored in New York, Pilmore in Philadelphia, and Strawbridge in Maryland. Wesley sent out to America Francis Asbury and Richard Wright, 1771. First Conference held in Philadelphia July 4, 1773; 10 preachers, and 1,160 members in the whole American Methodist Church. In 1774 there were 17 preachers and 1,073 members. Division of the Methodist Episcopal Church of the United States (1844) into the Methodist Episcopal Church and the Methodist Episcopal Church, South, on the question of slavery.

THE EVANGELICAL ASSOCIATION.

In 1796 Jacob Albright began preaching the Gospel to the neglected Germans of eastern Pennsylvania. A meeting of his converts in 1800 chose him as their pastor, or bishop, and gave him jurisdiction as such over the classes. In 1805 the first conference assembled, and in 1816 a general conference, consisting of all the elders, met at the house of M. Dreisbach in Union County., Penn. Since 1854, general conferences, consisting of delegates from annual conferences, have been held every four years. During its earlier years the Evangelical Association was violently opposed, but for the last fifty years it has been prosperous. As the Association denounced slavery it has made no progress in the southern states, but it has spread over the North and West, into Canada, Germany and

Switzerland. In polity, worship, and plans of work it resembles the Methodist Episcopal Church; the ministers are divided into elders and deacons: the bishops are elected by general conference for four years, and may be re-elected; the presiding elders are elected by the annual conferences also for four years, and may be re-elected. At first preaching and other public services were held exclusively in the German language; now, however, the English also is employed in about one-third of the Association. The denomination has a flourishing college at Naperville, Ill: a seminary at New Berlin, Pa.; a seminary at Reading, Pa.; also a seminary at Reutlingen, Germany; and one half interest in a seminary at Tokio, Japan. In 1884 it reports 24 annual conferences, 1615 preachers (itinerant and local), 1699 churches, 526 parsonages, 124,554 members, 2,234 Sunday-schools, with 23,626 teachers and 141,154 scholars. Nine missionaries are at work in Japan; and nearly 400 home missionaries are employed; the missionary contributions as reported for 1883 are $116,532.49.

UNITED BRETHREN IN CHRIST.

A Protestant church which arose among the Germans in Pennsylvania about 1760. In 1752 Philip William Otterbein, a missionary of the German Reformed Church, sent to America by the Synod of Holland, began to preach in Lancaster, Pa., but, becoming conscious that he was not converted he rested not until he realized the new birth. He held meetings for prayer and religious conference, and outside of his charge he held "great meetings." A special invitation to all who had experienced a change of heart was given to one of these. A large assembly of Lutherans, Reformed, Mennonites, Amish, and Moravians gathered and listened to a remarkably effective sermon by Martin Boehm, a Mennonite preacher. After the sermon Otterbein arose, embrached Boehm, and exclaimed, "We are brethren!"

This was the origin of the name. In 1800 the first annual conference met, and the first general conference in 1815. The Church is Arminian in theology, and supplies its congregations with preaching on the itinerant plan. Bishops are elected for a term of four years, and Presiding Elders for a term of one year. In 1881 the denomination had 47 annual conferences, 4,524 churches, 5 bishops, 2,196 ministers, 157,835 members, with a publishing house at Dayton, O., and 13 educational institutions in various parts of the United States. Foreign missions have been established in Africa and Germany. Until 1825 the Church labored principally among Germans, but now a large part of its membership use the English language.

SOCIETY OF FRIENDS.

This body of Christians, better known as Quakers, was founded in England in 1647 by George Fox. Their leading doctrine is the "internal light" of the Holy Spirit. They worship as they believe themselves to be moved by the Spirit. They regard an educated and salaried ministry, the taking of oaths, engaging in war, stage plays and amusements, slavery, etc., as inconsistent with Scriptural religion. About the year 1827, Elias Hicks, originated a schism which led about one half of the Society in America to deny the miraculous conception, divinity and atonement of Christ and the authenticity and divine authority of the Scriptures. These were called the Hicksite Friends. Out of opposition to this movement there arose a new sect called "Wilburites," after their leader, John Wilbur.

MENNONITES.

This church was organized in the 16th century, in Switzerland, by Simon Menno. They believed in the personal reign of Christ on earth during the millennium, in the unlawfulness of oaths, of war, of lawsuits, of resisting violence and wrong, and of allowing civil magistrates to be members of the Church. Their doctrines resembled those of the reformed churches. Menno's stringent discipline soon produced divisions. Persecution caused them to scatter abroad. For years they were given refuge in Russia, but in 1871 the attitude of the government changed toward them, and emigration to the United States was begun, where, besides the main body there exist four minor sects of Mennonites. The Dutch Mennonites have a theological seminary at Amsterdam. The denomimation also has a publishing house at Elkhart, Ind. Their bishops, deacons and ministers are chosen by lot, and meet in semi-annual district conferences.

DENOMINATIONAL CHURCH STATISTICS.

Name of Denomination.	Churches (Organizations, not buildings).	Ministers (Local Preachers not included).	Communicants or Members.
Adventists:			
Adventists	91	107	11,100
Second	583	501	63,500
Seventh Day	680	165	18,168
Baptists:			
(Regular)	27,913	17,327	2,474,771
Disciples of Christ (Campbellites)	5,700	4,050	631,720
German Baptists (Tunkers or Dunkards)	500	1,731	80,000
Free-will Baptists	1,367	1,257	78,909
Anti-Mission Baptists	1,802	918	46,507
Church of God (Winebrennarians)	475	450	45,000
Seventh Day Baptists	100	120	8,800
Six Principle Baptists	17	15	2,189
General Baptists	800	300	13,000
Christians (often called Christ-yans)	2,000	1,500	150,000
Christian Union Churches of the West	100	100	100,000
Congregationalists	4,016	3,795	397,630
Episcopalians:			
Protestant	2,933	3,559	364,003
Reformed	80	86	7,481
Friends (Orthodox)	300	880	68,000
Friends (Hicksites, so-called)	272	150	29,845
Lutherans	6,327	3,552	800,189
Mennonites	410	250	50,000
Methodists:			
Methodist Episcopal Church (North)	18,152	12,654	1,799,593
" " " (South)	15,465	4,045	879,299
African M. E. Church	4,000	1,832	391,044
African M. E. Zion Church	3,729	2,061	300,000
United Brethren in Christ	4,292	1,246	161,828
Colored M. E. Church	1,856	1,051	145,000
Methodist Protestant Church	1,838	1,400	125,671
Welsch Calvinistic Methodists	1,147	600	118,979
Evangelical Association	1,699	958	124,554
Wesleyan Methodist Connection of Amer.	495	400	17,087
Free Methodists	922	461	14,250
Independent Methodists	40	24	5,000
Primitive Methodists	84	44	3,585
Union American M. E. Church		112	3,500
African Union First Colored Meth. Ch	50	40	3,000
Congregational Methodists	120	100	13,000
New Jerusalem Church (Swedenborgian)	93	96	5,000
Presbyterians:			
Northern	5,858	5,218	600,695
Southern	2,040	1,070	127,017
Cumberland	2,591	1,436	113,750
United	839	717	85,443
Synod of the Reformed Pres. Church	118	107	10,322
General Synod of the Ref. Pres. Church	60	50	5,000
Associate Ref. Synod of the South	180	76	6,737
Reformed Church U. S. A. (German)	1,467	783	169,530
Reformed Church in America (Dutch)	516	569	80,156
Unitarians	360	430	20,000
United Brethren in Christ	4,524	2,196	157,835
United Brethren (Moravians)	84	70	9,928
Universalists	719	713	86,238

AMERICAN FOREIGN MISSIONARY WORK.

The following figures show, as far as figures can do so, the present condition of the missionary work of American churches in foreign lands. Many important missions in European countries, which are considered Evangelical, are excluded. We believe the table will be found approximately correct as the reports of the various Societies and Boards will permit.

Denominations.	Foreign Missionary Revenue for latest year recorded.	Students and Scholars in Seminaries and Schools.	Communicants.	Ordained Native Ministers.	Total Native helpers.†	Total missionaries male and female.*	Ordained missionaries.
Congregational A. B. C. F. M.	$590,996	35,625	19,364	144	1,827	433	154
Am. Baptist Missionary Union	307,195	14,137	50,691	173	686	193	78
F. M. B. Southern Baptists	56,905		1,022		26	40	15
Free Baptists	14,517	3,089	551		14	14	6
Lutherans	43,263	716	2,767	5	205	11	9
Methodist Episcopal, North	362,398	12,693	20,095	246	1,845	187	103
" South	150,971	1,497	2,796	36	104	34	22
Protestant Episcopal	158,930	1,525	1,190	38	145	48	16
Presbyterian, Northern	655,588	21,253	17,366	92	810	446	160
" Southern	69,071	502	1,700	15	56	50	23
United Presbyterian	102,839	4,531	1,906	11	211	52	11
Reformed "	16,422	648	130		43	9	3
Cumberland "	10,185		35		6	5	2
Reformed (Dutch)	65,285	2,183	2,843	20	135	44	20
Evangelical Association	17,303	132	146		7	9	3
Other Denominations not enumerated	82,697	168	984		93	94	27
Totals	$2,704,565	98,699	123,586	781	6,213	1,666	652

* This includes medical missionaries and teachers.
† including ordained native ministers.

GENERAL RELIGIOUS STATISTICS.

According to the recently published statistics of the religious status of the world. There are 425,000,000 Christians on the globe, who are divided into 215,000,000 Roman Catholics, 122,000,000 Protestants, 80,000,000 adherents of the Greek Church and 8,000.000 of other Churches. In the German Empire there were, on Dec. 1st, 1880 (the last time that general statistics were taken), 28,318,592 Evangelical Christians, 16,-229,290 Roman Catholics, 93,834 other Christians, 561,612 Jews, and 30,675 adherents of other religions. The other Protestant countries of Europe are England, the Low Countries, Sweden and Norway, Denmark and Switzerland. In Austria-Hungary there are 28,500,000 Catholics, and a little over 3,500,000 Protestants; in France, 37,000,000 Catholics and 600,000 Protestants; in Russia 8,000,000 Catholics, 4,000,000 Protestants, 63,000,000 Greek Christians, 2,500,000 Jews and 2,000,000 Mohammedans; in Italy there are 28,500,000 Catholics and only 60,000 Protestants; in Sweden, over 4,500,000 Protestants but only 600 Catholics; in Denmark, 1,953,000 Protestants and 3,000 Catholics; in Switzerland 1,670,000 Protestants and 1,160,-000 Catholics; in Belgium, 5,500,000 Catholics and 15,000 Protestants; in the Netherlands, 2,500,000 Protestants and 1,450,000 Catholics. For England the following figures are given: 18,537,-000 members of the State Church, 1,473,000 of the Scotch Church, 6,039,000 Dissenters, 5,520,000 Catholics and 76,000 Israelites.

INDEX

	Page.
INTRODUCTION	3

Political State of the World at Christ's Birth.— Religious State of the World at Christ's Birth.— Political State of Judæa at Christ's Birth.— Religious State of the Jews at Christ's Birth.

CHAPTER I.—*The First Century* 7

The Life of Christ.— First Year of the Church.— Progress of the Gospel.— Caligula.— The Church at Antioch.— Call of the Gentiles.—Death of James.—The Service of the Gentiles.—Dispersion of the Apostles.—St. Paul's Apostolic Journeys.—Judaizing Christians.— Council at Jerusalem.— Cerinthus.— Disagreement between Paul and Peter.—Nero.—St. Paul's Imprisonment.— St. Paul's Release.— Christianity at Rome.— Christianity at Alexandria.— Freedom from Roman Persecution.— Causes of Roman Persecution. — First General Persecution.— Effects of Persecution.— The Jewish War.—The Christians at Pella.— Nazarenes and Ebionites.— Titus. — Domitian. — The Nicolaitan Heresy.—Nerva.—The Apostle John.

CHAPTER II.—*From the Death of John the Evangelist till the Rise of Monachism* 26

Third Persecution.—Millennium.—Saturninus.—Basilides.— Hadrian.—Fourth General Persecution.—Apologies of Quadratus and Aristides.—Hadrian's Decree.—Antoninus Pius.—Valentinus.—Cerdon and Marcion.—Justin Martyr,— Edict of Antoninus Pius.—Marcus Aurelius.—Fifth General Persecution.— Martyrdom of Polycarp.— Montanus and his Schism.— Bardisanes and his Heresy. — Persecution of Lyons and Vienne.— Irenæus.— Christianity in Britain.— Commodus.— Severus.— Heresy of Theodotus and Artemon.— The Patripassians.—Tertullian.— Sixth General Persecution.— Origen.—Persecution at Rome.— Rapid Succession of Roman Emperors.— Alexander Severus.— Council of Iconium.— Maximinus.— Seventh General Persecution.—Gordian.— Heresy of Beryllus.— Philip.— Cyprian.—Decius.—Eight General Persecution.—Monachism.

INDEX.

Page.

CHAPTER III.—*From the Rise of Monachism till the Council at Nice*..... 47

    Gallus.—Valerian.—Ninth General Persecution.—Infant Baptism.—The Sabellian Heresy.—Gallienus.—Paulianists.—Gregory Thaumaturgus.—Aurelian.—Manichæism.—Diocletian.—The Hieracites.—The Meletian Schism.—Tenth General Persecution.—The Donatists.—Conversion of Constantine.—Subsequent Acts of Constantine.—Arianism.—The Council of Nice.—Bishops in the Early Church.—Heretics.—Apologists.—Persecutions.—Apostolic Fathers.—Church Fathers.

CHAPTER IV.—*From the Council at Nice till the Birth of Martin Luther*.. 61

    Death of Constantine.—Julian.—Arianism.—The Roman See.—Pelagianism.—Abuses.—The English Church.—Mohammedanism.—Gregory the Great.—The Venerable Bede.—Reign of Charlemagne.—Controversies.—Hildebrand, or Gregory VII.—The Papal Power in England.—Declension of Papal Supremacy.—Papal Claims to Authority.—Monks and Friars.—The Waldenses and Albigenses.—The Inquisition.—John Wicliffe.—John Huss.—Burning of Heretics.—Reginald Pecock.—The Pragmatic Sanction, and the Concordat.—Ecclesiastical Abuses.

CHAPTER V.—*From the Birth of Martin Luther till the Bible was set up in the Churches* 82

    Martin Luther.—Accession of Henry VIII.—Election of Bishops.—Pope Leo X.—Indulgencies.—Luther, and the Reformation of Germany.—Diet of Augsburg.—Reformers.—German Reformers.—Swiss Reformers.—Order of Jesuits.—The Reformation in England.—Submission of the Clergy.—Henry marries Anne Boleyn.—Renunciation of Papal Authority.—Persecution.—Fall of Queen Anne Boleyn.—Instructions for a Visitation of the Monasteries.—Dissolution of the lesser Monasteries.—Demolition of Becket's Shrine.—Dissolution of the larger Monasteries.—The Six Articles.

CHAPTER VI.—*From the Time the Bible was set up in the Churches till James I. Ascended the Throne*.. 98

    The Bible set up in the Churches.—Queen Catherine Parr.—The King's Primer.—Death of Martin Luther.—Death of Henry VIII.—Accession of Edward VI.—Images.—Visitation of the Clergy.—First Book of Homilies.—Repeal of the Six Articles.—Cranmer's Catechism.—Book of Common Prayer.—Sacerdotal Vestments.—Altars.—Revision of the Book of Common Prayer.—Articles of Religion.—Death of Edward.—The Reign

Page.

of Mary.— Reconciliation with Rome.— Distinguished Marian Martyrs.— Death of Mary.— The Reign of Elizabeth.—The Act of Supremacy.— Consecration of Parker. — Jewel's Challenge and Apology.—Rise of Puritanism.—Persecution of the Huguenots.— The Prophesyings.— The Three Articles.—The Council of Trent.—Extension of Protestantism.

CHAPTER VII.—*From the Accession of James I. till the Present Time*... 118

The Hampton Court Conference.— Synod of Dort.— Archbishop Laud.—The Star Chamber.—Fifth Monarchy Men.— The Savoy Conference.—Final Revision of the Liturgy.—Spread of Protestantism.—Wesley, and the English Methodism.— The Virginia Colony.— Protestant Episcopal Church.— Reformed Episcopal Church.— The Puritans in America.— Congregationalism.— Reformed Church.— The Baptists.— German Reformed Church.— The Lutheran Church.— The Presbyterians.— The Methodists in America.—The Evangelical Association.—United Brethren in Christ.— Society of Friends.— Mennonites.— Denominational Church Statistics.— American Foreign Missionary Work.— General Religious Statistics.

www.ingramcontent.com/pod-product-compliance
Lightning Source LLC
Chambersburg PA
CBHW020055170426
43199CB00009B/293